RUDYARD

1797-1997

THE BI-CENTENNIAL HISTORY

by

BASIL JEUDA

Published by

CHURNET VALLEY BOOKS

43 Bath Street
Leek
Staffordshire
01538 399033

© Basil Jeuda and Churnet Valley Books
1997

ISBN 1897949 30 8

A delightful view of Rudyard Lake c1993, looking north with Bosley Cloud in the background. Bottom left can be seen the piecemeal development at Harper's Gate and along Lake Road. Centre left is the Hotel Rudyard, with its grounds sloping down to the Feeder, behind which, on higher ground, lies the caravan park attached to Spite Hall. Behind Spite Hall, slightly to the left, is Horton Lodge Special School, with Fairview, now a nursing home, situated immediately behind. Along the western (left) side of the lake, several boathouses can be seen, with the 'Lady of the Lake' jutting out. The far end of the lake, to the left, was the location of the former Golf Course. The straight path leading from the Dam, to the bottom of the photograph is the track of the former Churnet Valley Railway.   *Horton Lodge Special School*

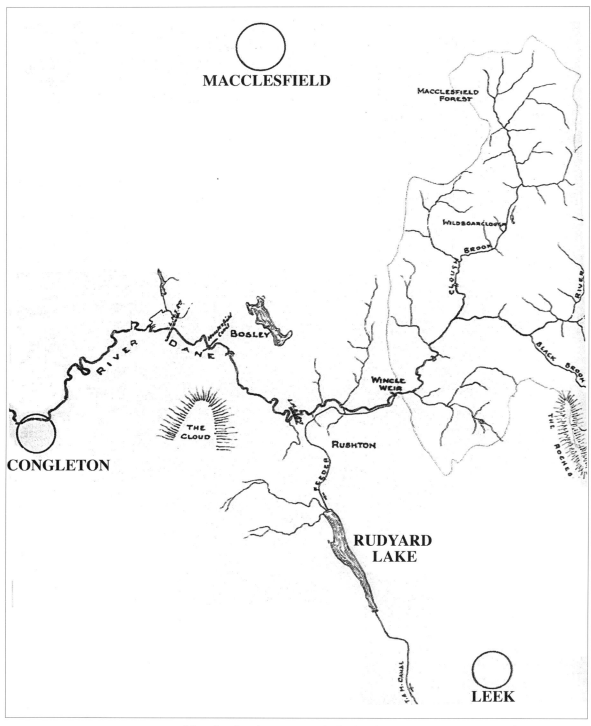

Map showing the water supply Rudyard Lake

British Waterways Board

INTRODUCTION

The Bi-centenary of Rudyard Lake, which occurs in 1997, provides the opportunity for an historical assessment of the contribution the lake has made, over its 200 years, to the industrial, economic and social development of the villages of Rudyard and Horton, of the nearby town of Leek, and of the Potteries and further afield.

In the Saxon era the village of Rudyard was known variously as Rodehyerd and Rudierd. In the Domesday Book of 1086, King William the Conqueror was tenant of the area, which was nearly all woodland and wasteland. Ranulph Rodehyerd, the great grandson of Richard the Crusader, received the grant of waste land of Gun Hill in 1318 from Nicholas, Abbot of Dieulacress. This area of Rodehyerd was, at this early period, attached to the Bishop of Chester's vast forested hunting lands.

Moving forward several hundred years, the two Rudyard sisters, Margaret and Mercy, sold the accumulated Rudyard estates to the Earl of Macclesfield in 1723 and these estates contained such properties as Rudyard Hall (418 acres), Green Tree (208 acres), Green Farm (180 acres), Barnswood (178 acres), Willgate (158 acres), and Hunt House (143 acres). These properties were part of the auction of 2082 acres of agricultural property which took place on Wednesday 9 July 1919, on the instructions of the Earl of Macclesfield. The 17th century Rudyard Hall is the oldest surviving building, together with the sites occupied by Barnswood (early 17th century), Hunt House Farm (by 1636), Willgate Farm (by 1669) and Highgate Farm (by 1677).

It was the passing of three different Enclosure Acts - Rushton James in 1772, Rushton Spencer in 1776 and Horton in 1815 - which determined village boundaries, with Rudyard becoming part of the Parish of Horton. In 1801 Rudyard had a population of 109. In 1834 Rudyard was classed as a small township, located between the course of Dunsmore Brook, which formerly ran down the centre of the lake, and Rudyard Hall and Barnswood, on the east side of the Macclesfield to Leek Road, located some 2$\frac{1}{2}$ miles north west of Leek.

Horton itself was a small village 3 miles west north west of Leek, with two townships; Horton with Horton Hay and Blackwood with Crowborough. Surviving properties, mainly farmhouses, date back a long way, for example, Horton Hall (by 1647), Reacliffe House (by 1675), Barnslee (by 1727), whilst there is a date stone of 1610 on what is now the Poacher's Tavern, but which was formerly known as the Railway Inn, then the Railway Hotel and then as the Station Hotel. By 1851 Rudyard covered 4,860 acres and had a population of 967. The point at which the road from Longsdon to Biddulph Moor intersected with the road from Pool End, on the Leek to Macclesfield Road, is at Harper's Gate, and it is in this area that the oldest surviving cottage properties are to be found. The significant expansion in residential property over the last 125 years had been in the Harper's Gate area, in what was and is Horton Parish but is now more popularly known as Rudyard. It is located on the south western tip of the former Rudyard township. As a result of the review of local government boundaries in 1934, parts of the former Horton parish were transferred to Endon and to Biddulph; the remainder was added to the parish of Rudyard, which was subsequently renamed Horton. For all these reasons, it has become very difficult to establish the growth in Rudyard's population over the years.

The origins of the Rudyard Reservoir, as it was more frequently known until the North Staffordshire Railway attempted to exploit it commercially for purposes other than as a reservoir in 1850, lay in the need for the Trent and Mersey Canal Company to provide, for its expanding canal system and for its growing commercial traffic, an increasing and continuous supply of water to enable narrow boats to pass through the numerous locks. The Company constructed reservoirs at Stanley and Knypersley to feed into the Caldon branch of the Trent and Mersey Canal at Endon during the 1780s, but these were still insufficient to meet the need. Eventually, in 1797, the Canal Company secured Parliamentary powers to construct the reservoir.

This book attempts to describe the changes in the 164 acre lake itself, and the changes in the ways in which it has been used and enjoyed; all this has had an inevitable impact on the physical development of Rudyard and Horton over the years, the growth in population, the growth and decline in tourism, the construction of villa residences, of boathouses, and of other houses and their subsequent change of use.

I was first drawn to study Rudyard through my long standing interest in the history of the North Staffordshire Railway Company. The NSR acquired the Canal Company, and through it, the reservoir, in 1847. Rudyard, and particularly the area around Harper's Gate, was a village which the North Staffordshire Railway, through its ownership of the lake, sought to shape and develop from the opening of its Churnet Valley Railway in 1849, right through to the termination of its separate existence in 1923. Since that date, under the successive ownership of the London Midland & Scottish Railway and British Waterways, the lake has continued to fulfil its original objectives as a reservoir for the canal system, whilst at the same time providing the opportunity for a variety of water-related sports.

Also by Basil Jeuda:

The Leek, Caldon & Waterhouses Railway	1980
Macclesfield, Bollington & Marple Railway	1983
Railways of the Macclesfield District	1984
Memories of the North Staffordshire Railway	1986
Railway Postcard Scenes of Cheshire	1987
Rudyard Lake Golf Club, 1906-1926	1993
Railways of Macclesfield	1995
The Knotty - an Illustrated History of the North Staffordshire Railway	1996

William Brookes of Willgate Farm, talking to Edgar Chapman of Leek, the driver of a De Dion Bouton, 1905, single cylinder model, belonging to Dr J M Johnson of Stockwell Street, Leek, at the bottom of the bank leading from Rudyard station to the Station Hotel. The Hotel is visible on the left and Rock House, partly obscured by cottages, and Holly Bank can be seen in the background. *George Bowyer collection*

ACKNOWLEDGMENTS

Many people have helped to make this book possible and I would like to thank the following: British Waterways Board at Northwich and Gloucester, Horton Parish Council, Horton Church Council, Keele University Library, the Leek Post and Times, the Public Record Office at Kew, and the William Salt Library at Stafford for access to their records; George Bowyer, Derek Bowcock, Alice Boulton, Robert Cartwright, Christine Chester, Fred & Joan Cooper, Alan Hancock and the British Trust for Ornithology, Vic Leese, George Lovenbury, Jim Ridgway, David Salt and Frank Sutton; Camera Five Four and Tim Shuttleworth for their photographic support; Rudyard residents past and present for their memories and access to their memorabilia, and Christine Pemberton for processing the text, for the design and layout and for her advice and contributions. I have acknowledged separately the many people who have so generously allowed me to reproduce their photographs and plans.

I would like to thank the Britannia Building Society, the Rudyard Lake Trust and Rudyard Lake Ltd for their generous sponsorship. My appreciation is also extended to Churnet Valley Books for their enthusiasm to publish it. Finally, I would like to thank my wife, Laura, for the continued support she gives to my historical research.

Basil Jeuda
Macclesfield
February 1997

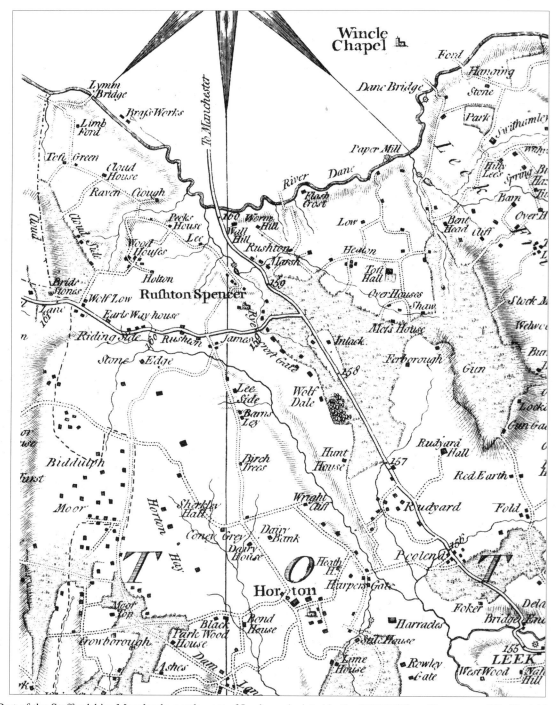

Part of the Staffordshire Moorlands, north west of Leek, as depicted in the 1776 William Yates map of Staffordshire. The reservoir was constructed on either side of Dunsmore Brook, with the north end just beyond a line connecting Barns Ley with Wolf Dale, and the south end slightly north of a line between Harper's Gate and Pool End. Running across the top of the map the River Dane can be seen, source of the future water for the reservoir, linked by a feeder constructed in 1809 just east of Rushton Marsh.

David Salt collection

CHAPTER 1
Rudyard Before the Lake to 1797

The origins of Rudyard Reservoir, as it will be described, until the coming of the railway in 1849, can be found in the promotion of a 1766 Act of Parliament, to link the River Trent at Wilden Ferry, near Derby, with the River Mersey near Runcorn, *"whereby an easy communication will be made between the two great port Towns of Hull and Liverpool."*

There was opposition from a rival scheme linking Witton Brook with Manchester, but the Trent and Mersey Canal bill received Royal Assent on 14 May 1766. Under this Act the Trent and Mersey Canal could be supplied from *"such Springs as shall be found in making the canal and from such Brooks ..... as shall be found within the distance of five hundred yards from any part of the canal and within the distance of five miles ...... between the first lock in Cheshire and the first lock in Staffordshire and also to make such reservoirs as shall be necessary"*.

In 1769, the Trent and Mersey Canal Company entered into an agreement with several landowners in the Caldon area of the Staffordshire Moorlands for *"the inexhaustible fund of limestone"*. The Caldon Canal, linking the limestone quarries with the Trent and Mersey Canal at Etruria, was considered as early as 1769, but as late as 1773 inclined places were intended instead of canal locks for moving tug boats, capable of carrying 5 tons, between the quarry and Froghall. In 1776 an Act of Parliament was obtained to build a canal from Etruria to Froghall, and a railway from Froghall to Caldon.

In the following years, the increase in traffic using the Caldon Canal was such that further sources of water had to be secured to prevent the canal from drying up. Reservoirs to serve the summit of the canal were built at Knypersley in 1782/83, at Stanley Pool and at Bagnall Reservoir in 1786/89. Despite this, both the Caldon and the Trent and Mersey Canals suffered from a general shortage of water in every year between 1788 and 1796, and in 1785 and 1795 all the reservoirs and even the Caldon Canal itself were *"drawn completely out"*.

One alternative to increase the supply of water to the summit level of the Caldon branch at Endon was through the construction of a canal from the top level of the Peak Forest Canal at Marple, via Macclesfield and Rudyard to Endon. Amongst the opponents to the scheme was the Trent and Mersey Canal Company, who saw it as a threat to its own plan for a branch from the Caldon Canal to Leek, which the Company was promoting, along with a feeder there to a reservoir at Rudyard. Although this Parliamentary bill failed, it was reintroduced in the 1796/97 session and secured Parliamentary approval in March 1797.

In 1791, William Arnett of Bank House, Rudyard, opened his home for preaching and a society was formed there. The procedure in those days was for a Methodist minister to call on the local society, examine the standards of faith and conduct and, if satisfied, he would appoint a class leader to supervise the spiritual oversight of the members. The Methodists of Bank House still continued their association with Horton Parish Church, their own meeting being held on week nights. By 1810 the society had six members; Joseph Bailey (leader), William Arnett, Mary Arnett, George Rogers, Mrs Hargreaves and Elizabeth Bailey. In 1813, Thomas Arnett entered the Wesleyan ministry. By 1844 ill health had forced him to become a supernumerary and he died in 1864.

Towards the end of 1811, the Trustees of Harper's Gate Chapel purchased an acre of land on the eastern side of Lake Road and planning permission was obtained for the erection of a new chapel. One of the conditions was that it should be built ten yards back from the road.

Horton Hall c1925

George Bowyer collection

Willgate farmyard 1919

Ivan Nixon collection

Rudyard Hall, west front, 1919

Ivan Nixon collection

Green Tree Farm 1919

Ivan Nixon collection

John Haworth, who built Cliffe Park Hall in 1811 at an estimated cost of £25,000.   *Christine Chester collection*

John Rennie 1769-1821, adviser to the Trent and Mersey Canal Company

Cliffe Park Hall, a 1904 view, taken at the time of its sale by descendants of the Haworth family to the North Staffordshire Railway for use as a hotel. From 1908 to 1926 it was the Club House of the Rudyard Lake Golf Club.   *George Bowyer collection*

CHAPTER 2
1797-1849

The construction of the dam commenced in 1797, with Hugh Henshall as resident engineer and John Rennie as consultant. Rennie's specifications for the Rudyard Dam are contained in his notes of 30 November 1797, and cover no fewer than thirteen items.

The first stipulates that *"The embankment must be made in the form of an horizontal arch, having a versed sine of 45 feet, to be 40 feet wide at the top. The back slope as 2 horizontal to 1 perpendicular, the face slopes as 5 horizontal to 3 perpendicular, thus the vase of the back on the dam will be 167 feet wide, and there must be a puddle in its middle 12 feet thick at bottom and 6 feet at top."*

The eleventh specification states that *"The face of the bank for the height of 4 feet above and about 6 feet below water level, should be covered with rubble stone to prevent the banks from receiving injury by the lash of the waves, these stones should be rammed into the face of the bank until the water has sufficiently mixed them with soil to lay firm."*

Initially, there were difficulties in deciding where the head or embankment of the proposed reservoir in Rudyard Vale should be located. In August 1797 John Rennie inspected the ground set out by Mr Cross for the embankment of the reservoir at Rudyard Vale. He reported in his Letter Book, dated 20 November 1797, that *"The situation chosen by him was certainly a proper one for obtaining as great a capacity as the vale would conveniently permit; but on trying the ground I found it so extremely porous in the sides and soft in the bottom that I judged it a very improper place to fix the head or dam of so extensive a reservoir. On searching further down the vale, the ground appeared worse; but at the distance of 330 yards higher up I found a very good situation, the sides being marl and the bottom a soft clay. I therefore fixed on this as the proper place for the dam and had it set out for execution accordingly. By this alteration the reservoir will be lessened in capacity by about ten acres, supposing the land already purchased only to be covered with water, which I think will be sufficient for the purposes wanted".*

The Dam was completed in 1800 by the contractors, Thomas Peak and John Mansfield, the resident engineer being James Potter. The branch canal to Leek appears to have been undertaken after the reservoir was completed. John Rennie made a final tour of inspection in March 1801 and shortly afterwards the canal opened, bringing with it the much needed water for the Leek and Caldon Canals; the feeder channel to Leek was 2½ miles long.

Because of the increasing demand placed on all the reservoirs serving the canals, it soon became clear that reliance on streams for providing water for the Rudyard reservoir was misplaced; between 1799 and 1807 the reservoir was full only once. The opening of the Uttoxeter Canal in 1811, from Froghall to Uttoxeter, with its many locks, only served to worsen the situation and, in anticipation of this, the Trent and Mersey Canal Company took powers under an 1809 Act of Parliament to make a feeder from the River Dane *"between.... Dane Bridge and the Paper Mill ..... and there erect a weir twelve inches above the Weir of the Paper Mill to receive from Time to Time a part of the flood water."* The Rudyard reservoir would therefore only receive water when the River Dane overflowed the twelve inch wall built there.

The increase in traffic on the Trent and Mersey Canal led to the need for a second tunnel at Harecastle - in turn potentially increasing the need for even more water. John Rennie carried out an inspection of Rudyard reservoir in 1821 and recommended either an alteration of the feeder from the River Dane, or a diversion into the reservoir of surplus water from the River Churnet. Finally, an 1823 Act gave powers to the Canal Company to deepen the Dane feeder and lower the weir six inches.

Prior to the damming of the Vale, much of the land was owned by the Earl of Macclesfield and by Mr Henry Haworth of Hulme Walfield, near Congleton. It was the latter's son, John Haworth, who built the castellated mansion known as Cliffe Park, "well adapted for the residence of a family of station", and it was estimated at the time that not less than £25,000 was expended by John Haworth and his cousin, the Reverend James Bostock, in the construction and completion of the mansion and the landscaping of the grounds, some 200 yards from the lakeside. Before Cliffe Park was built, James Haworth and his mother, Mrs Sarah Bostock Haworth, lived at Reacliffe and Barnslea respectively. In 1831, John Haworth died and his property passed on to his first cousin, Fanny Bostock, who had borne him an illegitimate daughter. The infant was placed in an orphanage.

The lake was commonly known as Rudyard Reservoir for about 35 years and during that period until 1850 it was used by the Trent and Mersey Canal exclusively for the purpose of supplying their canals - the Caldon and the Trent and Mersey - with water during dry weather; the rights to fishing, sporting and boating on the eastern side of the lake were exercised by the Earl of Macclesfield and on the western side by the Haworth/Bostock families, and this accounted for 80 or 90 acres out of the lake's total acreage, and they prevented others from shooting and fishing. These rights were strictly enforced by James Haworth and Fanny Bostock. Around 1826, some parties arrived with drag and stocking nets from Mr Antrobus, agent for the Earl of Macclesfield, and dragged without permission; cattle were watered and pastured at the reservoir at the same time, again without permission. Shortly after Fanny Bostock gained ownership of Cliffe Park, she warned off those who were fishing without permission, and exercised very strictly the game and fishing rights to Antrobus and to Mr Ward for two years, who occupied the Keepers House, and then to Mr James Tredwell, who was the contractor appointed by the NSR to construct the Churnet Valley line from North Rode to Uttoxeter.

James Haworth himself was not much of a sportsman; it was recalled that he had gone up to the parties at the reservoir and *"he would have put them in the pool very soon"*. The lake was the *"resort of huge quantities of wildfowl and wild ducks, plovers, wood gooses, snipe and woodcock."* After the lake was created and stocked with fish, Mrs Haworth sent men fishing with nets, and the first time the nets were cast 200 lbs of fish were caught. Later, trout, tench, pike, perch and a few carp were landed, with the pike weighing as much as 16lb.

The North Staffordshire Railway Act enabling the railway line to be built alongside Rudyard lake received Royal Assent on 26 June 1846. The contractors appointed by the NSR were J&S Tredwell, and they commenced construction at Leek on 21 September 1847, and in the Rudyard area on 11 October 1847. Whilst the NSR initially built stations on the Churnet Valley line at Bosley, Rushton, Leek, Cheddleton, Froghall, Oakamoor, Alton and Uttoxeter, when it opened in July 1849 there was controversy as to where, if at all, a station should be built to serve Rudyard, Harper's Gate and Horton. Fanny Bostock had used considerable exertion to fix the location of the station to serve the area at Rye Croft Gate, at the northern end of the lake; she was supported by local farmers, who offered to provide the requisite land free of charge and to fund the cost of a station and a goods warehouse, which would have served a population of nearly 3,000 people. Instead, a memorial was presented to the NSR on behalf of the landowners of 12,000 acres (including the Earl of Macclesfield and others) for a station at Harper's Gate; this was approved by the NSR on 14 August 1849, even though the community served was only around 600 persons. This decision was strategically important for the future development of Rudyard because, as Fanny Bostock claimed in her litigation, *"if the station had been at Rye Croft Gate, therefore Regattas would not have been successful because passengers would have been brought near the other end of the lake where the NSR has no lands to erect a public house, or celebrate amusements."*

Wesleyan Methodism within the Rudyard area had its origins at Harper's Gate in 1821. The services were originally held at the house of Mr Thomas Arnett at Bank Top; when he was removed to another part of the country the services were continued at Harracles Mill until 1854. Services were part of the Leek circuit, when it was separated from the Burslem circuit. Early in the 19th century, the entire area of the circuit was covered with Methodist centres; most of these were farmhouses, where services were held fortnightly and monthly, with two or three places grouped together.

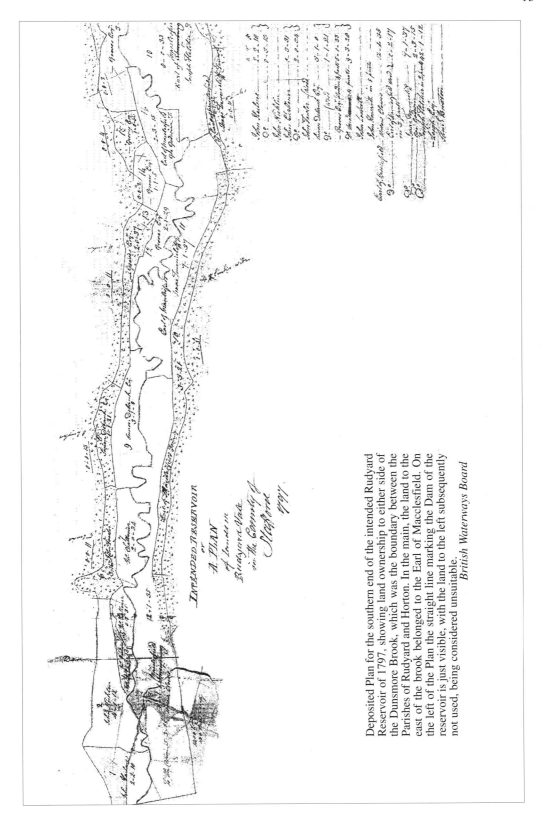

Deposited Plan for the southern end of the intended Rudyard Reservoir of 1797, showing land ownership to either side of the Dunsmore Brook, which was the boundary between the Parishes of Rudyard and Horton. In the main, the land to the east of the brook belonged to the Earl of Macclesfield. On the left of the Plan the straight line marking the Dam of the reservoir is just visible, with the land to the left subsequently not used, being considered unsuitable.

British Waterways Board

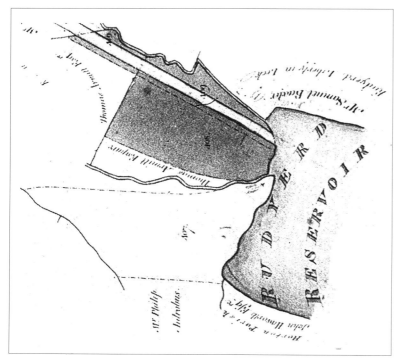

The Trent and Mersey Canal Company's 1816 estate plan, showing the north end of Rudyard reservoir. The line of the feeder from the River Dane is clearly visible at the top of the plan.
British Waterways Board

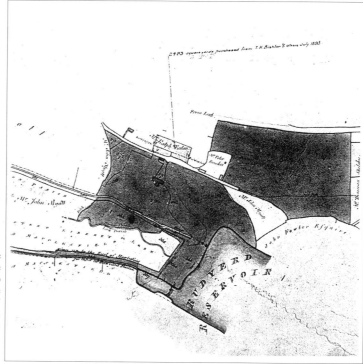

The 1816 estate plan, showing the southern end of Rudyard reservoir. The line of the feeder from the Reservoir to the Leek canal is clearly visible in the centre, above which can be seen the "T" shape of Phillips Hay, the residence of the water bailiff, which later, in 1850, became an ale house and then the Hotel Rudyard.
British Waterways Board

A delightful view, looking east, of the Feeder Cottage in the Dane Valley c1903. This was occupied for over 100 years by one of two bailiffs looking after Rudyard Lake, the other living at Phillips Hay and from 1852 onwards, Reservoir House at the south end of Rudyard Lake. Feeder Cottage ceased to be occupied by a water bailiff in 1959 but was not sold by the British Waterways until 1995.   *Author's collection*

A delightful 1908 view of Edwardian ladies punting on the Dane feeder.

Author's collection

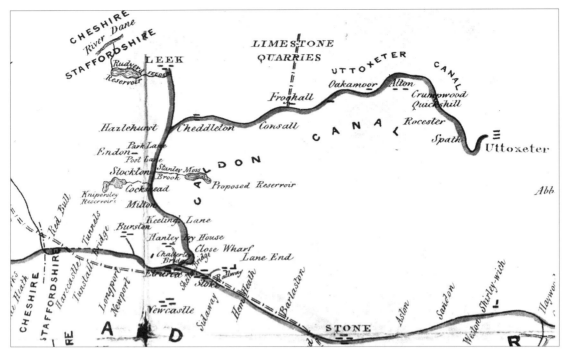

1838 map showing the canal system of North Staffordshire, with the short Leek Canal branching off the Caldon Canal at Hazelhurst and the Uttoxeter Canal extending to Froghall. Top left shows how Rudyard reservoir feeds into the Leek Canal, whilst across the bottom of the map can be seen the section of the Trent and Mersey Canal from Great Haywood to Harecastle and Red Bull. *David Salt collection*

Above:
Packsaddle Cottage 1919. *Ivan Nixon collection*
Right:
John Bowyer c1860, who farmed at Packsaddle Hollow, Rudyard. *William Salt Library*

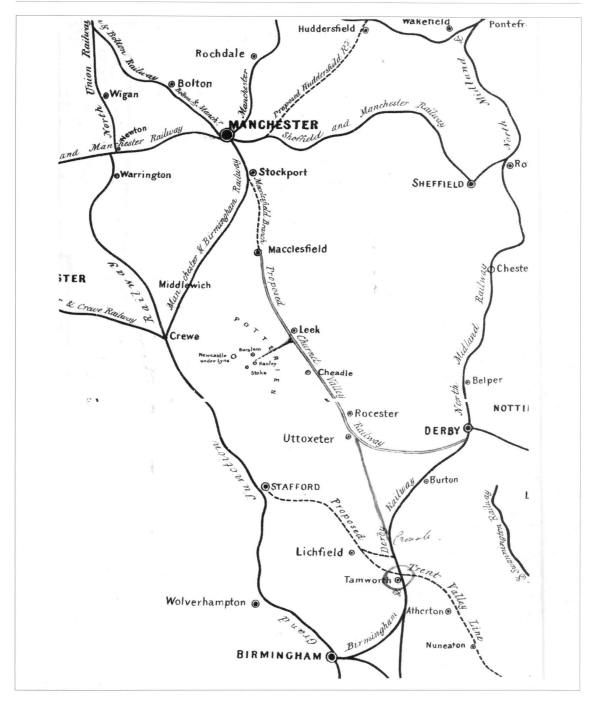

1844 Plan, deposited by the promoters of the Churnet Valley Railway, which was intended to run from Macclesfield, via Leek, to Derby. The line of the intended railway in earlier 1840 and 1841 schemes passed to the east but immediately adjacent to Rudyard Reservoir. This particular scheme was taken over by the North Staffordshire Railway in 1845 and was authorised to proceed by an Act of Parliament on 26 June 1846. *Author's collection*

Fanny Bostock, a portrait executed c1835. She inherited Cliffe Park Hall in 1831, on the death of her first cousin and lover, John Haworth. Fanny Bostock fought a five year long High Court action against the North Staffordshire Railway, from 1851 to 1856, and was ultimately successful in securing a permanent injunction preventing the Railway Company from using the lake for commercial advantage. It took an Act of Parliament in 1904 to overturn this.   *Christine Chester collection*

An early engraving reproduced in Sleigh's History of Leek 1883.

Advertisement for the 1873 Rudyard Ball, one of several initiatives in the early 1870s to attract visitors to the Rudyard Hotel.
Macclesfield Library

The earliest known photograph to have survived of Rudyard, taken c1868. This is a view of the Hotel Rudyard taken from the Feeder. The original water bailiff's house is in the foreground, with a later extension behind.
Author's collection

A view of the Earl of Macclesfield's boathouse, on the eastern side of the lake, also taken c1868, at the same time as the preceding photograph. This boathouse was built sometime between 1844 and 1868.
Author's collection

RUDYARD FETE AND REGATTA.

EASTER MONDAY,

Published this day in a neat wrapper, price 2d.
A GUIDE BOOK TO RUDYARD LAKE and ALTON TOWERS, descriptive of the Scenery and objects of interest on the Churnet Valley, North Staffordshire Railway.

Also, Price 3d, in a neat wrapper, the Authorised PROGRAMME OF THE DAY'S FESTIVITIES, including a full and correct list of upwards of 25 competing Boats, with the names and colours of the competitors,

A PROGRAMME and GUIDE, 4d.

May be had of the Booksellers, Messrs. SMITH and SONS, Railway.

This advertisement for what was to become the notorious Fête and Regatta at Rudyard on 21 April 1851 appeared in the Macclesfield Courier on 19 April 1851. The Guide Book, advertised here, was the first to be published covering both Rudyard Lake and Alton Towers - the two main tourist attractions on the Churnet Valley Railway line.

Macclesfield Library

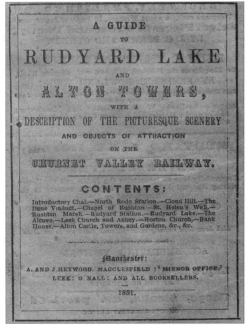

The front cover of the first ever guide book to Rudyard Lake and Alton Towers, published in April 1851, price 3d. It was produced in an effort to publicise the attractions offered by the Churnet Valley Railway. Peter Ullivero's advertisement for the Rudyard Lake Hotel is taken from inside the guide book. *Author's collection*

CHAPTER 3
1849-1889

The popularity of Rudyard and the lake, and the subsequent development of the neighbourhood, would not have been achieved without the proximity of the railway. The Churnet Valley line, which hugged the eastern bank of the lake, was one of a group of railway lines promoted by the NSR which secured Parliamentary approval on 26 June 1846. These particular lines were part of an emerging national network linking North West England with the East and West Midlands and London, whilst also linking the Potteries and neighbouring towns in Staffordshire and Cheshire into the national system.

During the 1830's, as numerous promoters brought forward competing schemes, some by-passing the Potteries and others including the Potteries, it became clear that the shortest and most direct route between Manchester and London was via Stockport, Macclesfield, Leek, Burton and Rugby; this particular route also had the advantage of linking the major manufacturing districts of Manchester with those of Derby. In 1836 the House of Commons resolved that the Churnet Valley line was *"highly desirable for the public interest"* and *"highly deserving of consideration in a future session"*.

One of the early railway schemes for this route was considered by the Manchester South Union Railway Company who, in the early part of 1836, commissioned a traffic census of coach traffic between Leek and London as part of an evaluation of this route. Whilst the MSURC did not, in the end, proceed with this route, the Manchester & Derby Railway was promoted on 17 February 1840, passing through Macclesfield, Leek, Rocester and across country via Marston Montgomery to Derby. This scheme did not proceed in 1840 and an almost identical scheme was brought forward on 17 February 1841 - the Manchester & Derby Railway (Churnet Valley). *"The state of the trade and the present prospect of the times"*, which included the unsettled political climate of 1842, especially the Chartist Riots and the General Strike, acted as a brake on the promotion of railway schemes for two or three years.

The Churnet Valley scheme reappeared in the form of a prospectus on 8 June 1844 for the Churnet Valley Railway from Manchester, via Macclesfield, to Derby, with an authorised capital of £1 million; the line would be 46 miles long and form a direct line from Macclesfield to London; this scheme attracted substantial financial interest and shares in the CVR were quoted on the London Stock Exchange. The subsequent Board of Trade review, which examined other neighbouring schemes, led to the proposals for the NSR to be established and for it to promote the CVR as one of several railways it was to open between 1848 and 1850.

The first indication that the NSR was contemplating the establishment of a refreshment house at Rudyard was when its Traffic Committee discussed the letting of its property, the water bailiff's house, on 7 May 1850. An inspection was carried out which found that *"for a small outlay (not exceeding £50) the premises might be adapted to the reception of visitors and thereby bring traffic on the Railway, and that they had given orders for such outlay accordingly."* Work did not yet proceed on this conversion, but as an interim measure the water bailiff, Joseph Tunnicliffe, applied on 5 July 1850 for a license to *"sell excisable liquors by retail to be drunk or consumed in the House or Premises at the southwardly end of the Rudyard Reservoir belonging to the Trent and Mersey Navigation Company, now in my own occupation as their Tenant, together with the Stabling, Outbuildings and Land .... and which is not kept or used as an Inn, Alehouse or victualling house"*, in good time for the opening of the station, called Rudyard (for Horton), on 18 August 1850; excursion trips from Macclesfield to the Rudyard Lake were advertised at First Class 2/-, Second Class 1/6d and Third Class 1/-.

The use of the small cottage with very limited facilities was clearly unsatisfactory and the NSR was obviously at a disadvantage in providing refreshments to the crowds now able to take advantage of the new station to visit Rudyard. To reach the lake, excursionists had to pass two small public houses which lay almost opposite each other, one a long established alehouse which is now the Poacher's Tavern, the other at what is now the Post Office.

At the meeting of 8 October 1850 the NSR Traffic Committee looked again at the possibility of converting the water bailiff's house into an inn, and also the erection of a cottage for their labourers at Rudyard, at a total cost of £400, but by the end of December no decision had been reached and the prospective tenant, a Mr Ullivero, from Congleton, was becoming decidedly frustrated. In January 1851 the NSR came to a decision to let the house to him at a rent of £35 per annum for a specified period of years, subject to the necessary alterations not exceeding £250. Trade must have been good, initially, especially from the two regattas held in the spring of 1851, but the prolonged litigation - that will be dealt with shortly - must have been damaging for business and in March 1853 Ullivero indicated to the NSR that he wished to relinquish occupancy of the hotel as soon as possible and would wish to nominate a suitable replacement tenant. It was not until 1855 that the replacement tenant was found. This was a Mr Barnes of Fernes House, near Longnor, and he was offered the tenancy at the lower rent of £25 per annum, for a period of 7 years.

With the opening of the Churnet Valley line, passing through Rudyard Vale and alongside the delightful lake, it did not take the NSR long to assess the commercial potential of the lake as a visitor attraction, with the NSR as the only practical means of bringing in those visitors. In advance of the station opening in August 1850, the NSR constructed well laid out walks on the side of the lake opposite to the railway line, intersected by a lofty hill planted with fir trees. Seats were arranged along the walk-ways and near to the summit of the hill a pleasant rustic arbour was erected, using larch trees, This work was executed by Mr Nunns, a landscape gardener from Leek, who also superintended the laying out of the different walks around the vicinity of the lake.

The arrival of excursionists, however, was viewed with increasing concern by the local landowner and occupier of Cliff Park Hall, Miss Fanny Bostock. In July 1850, even before the station had opened, her brother, the Reverend James Bostock, wrote on her behalf to the NSR, alleging trespass on her property by a pleasure party conveyed by the NSR. In subsequent correspondence the NSR vigorously asserted that *"the land and water of the reservoir at Rudyard are the property of the NSR, and that neither the Company nor anyone acting under their authority have to their knowledge done anything exceeding their rights as owners."*

This antagonistic correspondence was the forerunner of litigation between Fanny Bostock and the NSR, which was precipitated by the holding of a regatta on the lake, organised by a Mr Weston of Manchester, and given every encouragement by the NSR. The regatta was one of two organised in 1851, the first being held on Easter Monday, 21 April 1851 and the second on Whit Monday 9 June 1851, and the litigation continued, as both Fanny Bostock and the NSR sought to protect what they both saw as their legitimate property rights, in expensive legal actions which lasted from July 1851 until February 1856, when the Vice-Chancellor's Court found in favour of Fanny Bostock.

On 19 April 1851 the NSR advertised a Grand Fête and Regatta on Rudyard lake for the following Easter Monday; the fête would consist of aquatic sports and archery contests, together with rustic sports and games, climbing matches and a maypole. Several marquees served refreshments and an iron steam boat plied for hire. There was also a military and brass band. Not surprisingly, this regatta proved a tremendous draw and attracted over 6,000 visitors. The Staffordshire Advertiser reported that *"there have been probably very few occasions when two or three distinct classes of artisans - the silk workers and dyers of Leek and Macclesfield, the cotton spinners and weavers of Lancashire and Cheshire and the potters, colliers and pitmen of Staffordshire - have been brought together in such vast numbers for the purposes of outdoor enjoyment and popular recreation."*

Fanny Bostock did not see it that way at all. She had complained to the NSR prior to the event. The noise began on Easter Sunday with the arrival of the iron steamer, commissioned by the NSR off Messrs Boulton of Ashton-under-Lyne; it had a locomotive type boiler and a non-condensing engine and was capable of carrying 60-70 passengers. According to John Cockayne, gamekeeper to John Cruso, who was a prominent solicitor in Leek, there was *"a great noise in thumping and hammering .... putting the steamer together, fitting materials so as to start it"*, and he observed the construction of it as being worked by a screw paddle. *"It created a violent commotion on the water, the water was all on the move."*

The subsequent evidence to the Court captured the flavour of the day. Extracts from George Bostock's evidence are particularly vivid:

*"People went to Cliffe Park and Reacliffe woods; people were running up and down, backwards and forwards among newly planted larch trees, and committed great damage. The crowd was very considerable and people were very noisy and disorderly, both in the boats and on the Bostock lands.........
I saw great numbers coming out of and going into the Bostock woods, rushing over and pulling down the stone wall dividing the Bostock's land from Miss Gaunt's - they were very low, disorderly persons."*

The disturbances were not merely on the day of the regatta. Peter Ullivero, tenant of the ale house, continued in the following weeks to offer boats for hire, and these boats plied all over the lake. Not only did some parties fish in front of the Bostock woods, but others came *"for some disgusting and improper purposes."* At the second regatta on the Whit Monday, trespass in the woods created further damage and on the Friday of that Whitsun week timber was cut and *"vast numbers of young larch, mountain ash and other trees of three years' growth were completely pulled up and destroyed."*

Shortly afterwards the case came for trial and in August 1851 the jury could not agree a verdict. A new trial started in London in February 1852, with the verdict in favour of Fanny Bostock. Nominal damages were awarded. Ever persistent, the NSR advertised another regatta on Whit Monday 1852, and Fanny Bostock sought and obtained an injunction which prevented it from being held. Litigation, thought to have cost Fanny Bostock £3,000, an enormous sum in those days, continued until February 1856, when the Court granted a perpetual injunction to restrain the NSR, firstly from holding any regatta on the reservoir, secondly from letting out boats for hire and thirdly, from using the reservoir to damage Fanny Bostock's interests, or for any other purposes than those sanctioned in Acts of Parliament. It was this decision that determined the use of the lake for the next fifty years. As this history unfolds, the ways in which the NSR sought to get round this injunction will become evident.

The immediate impact on holiday events at Rudyard was felt on Easter Monday 1852. On 17 April of that year the Staffordshire Advertiser reported thus; *"This lovely spot was not visited by any great number of persons upon this occasion, beautiful and tempting as was the weather. Those who did attend, however, came prepared to enjoy a sylvan day in a scene worthy of their admiration. The amusements were all of a quiet and orderly kind; some few joined in a dance with great glee, and acquitted themselves apparently greatly to their own satisfaction and enjoyment. Be it ever so."*

Mention should be made of Rudyard Kipling. His parents, John Lockwood Kipling and Alice Macdonald, met for the first time in the summer of 1863 at a picnic party at the lake. They became engaged and married, two years later, in London on 18 March 1865. Immediately after the wedding ceremony, the Kiplings sailed for India, where John was to take up an appointment as head of a new Art School in Bombay. Their first child was born in Bombay on 30 December 1865, and was christened Joseph (after his grandfather), Rudyard (in recognition of the place where his parents had first met). Thus the name of this little village in North Staffordshire was perpetuated for all time in the annals of English literature, for Rudyard Kipling was destined to become one of the foremost writers and poets of the later Victorian age, and was eventually awarded the Nobel prize for his contribution to literature.

Despite the injunctions, the NSR still continued, as best it could, to exploit the attractions of the lake and its surroundings. It was best able to achieve this over the next half century through the entrepreneurial endeavours of successive tenants of the NSR's Hotel Rudyard. A steady stream of Sunday school trips and works outings visited the hotel and walked around the lake, whilst the NSR would lay on special excursion trains and organise special events, though taking care at all times not to fall foul of the 1856 Court injunction.

The first major event, which took place with the consent of the Magistrates, was the appearance of the African Blondin, who on 26 September 1864 was engaged to cross Rudyard lake on a rope suspended 100 feet above the water. The NSR ran trains from the Potteries towns, and from Congleton, Macclesfield and Uttoxeter. The admission price was 6d and there were between three and four thousand spectators.

There was a band for dancing, a comic vocalist and a brilliant display of fireworks. This whole event passed off without incident, in marked contract to the Regatta and Fête of 1851.

1869 saw another change in the tenancy of the Hotel Rudyard, made attractive *"by the large business it is now doing and the ample additional accommodation that the NSR intends to provide".* In October 1869 tenders were invited for alterations to the Hotel. These were to be submitted to the Engineer's Office, Canal Department, at Stoke station. Mr Henry Platt of New Belle Vue, Basford, near Stoke-on-Trent took over the tenancy in 1870, with the hotel now enlarged by the addition of a large new wing containing a splendid ball room which provided ample accommodation should the weather prove unfit for outdoor recreation. A convenient archery and croquet ground was laid out, whilst other amusements such as swing boats, quoits, bowls and velocipedes were also provided. The new tenant was able to offer not only dinner, teas and other refreshments for *"Pic-nic Parties from 10 persons upwards"*, but also to provide *"standing ground for stalls, shows and shooting galleries."* Excursion trains ran on Saturdays, Mondays and Thursdays.

In 1871 Henry Platt promoted Rudyard's first Well Dressing, with a view to establishing an annual festival similar to that celebrated in several other places in Staffordshire and Derbyshire. The well, which was known to have existed for upwards of eighty years, was 30 feet deep, the bottom being approached by a winding flight of some ninety steps. By the turn of the century the Well Dressing ceremony had been discontinued. The well lies on the western bank of the dam end, near to the tourist informaton centre, and was cleaned and renovated by the Manpower Services Commission c1984.

As evidence of the growing popularity of Rudyard, a new ball room was opened at the Rudyard Hotel on 9 January 1873. A select company of fifty attended the ball, which commenced at 9pm and lasted until almost daylight. A special train ran from Stoke, with cabs conveying parties from the station to the Hotel.

The third annual Well Dressing, held on 16 June 1873, was extremely popular, with more than 6,000 people present; other entertainment included dance music, shooting galleries, archery, quoits, skittles and highland and Morris dancing. Unfortunately, many of the excursionists delayed their departure and, having missed the last train, had to 'tramp it' to Leek and to the Potteries, suffering great discomfort en route. The NSR encountered a great deal of criticism for not having run emergency trains.

The attractions of Rudyard were further enhanced with the opening, on 1 June 1876, of the Rudyard Skating Rink. Rinking, as it was called, had become a popular sport of the day and there were already nearby rinks in Newcastle and Hanley. A Macclesfield entrepreneur, Mr Joseph Thornley, built an 8,000 square feet roller skating rink using the finest Val de Travers asphalt. The rink was located at the rear of the Hotel Rudyard, where a number of trees had been cut down to provide space. There were three skating sessions daily and cheap railway excursions were run from the Potteries.

During 1876 improvements were made to the Dam to enhance its attraction for visitors. The first Grand Aquatic Fête to be held at Rudyard took place on Monday 25 June 1877. The fête took the form of several swimming competitions; a man and dog swimming race, the Beckwith family performing their amazing stunts of nautation, whilst Captain Webb gave a representation of his unique feat of swimming the Channel. The event was advertised as follows: *"The bathing costumes being full and complete, the most fastidious of either sex may, with propriety, be present at this Entertainment."*

A grandstand was erected to accommodate several hundred spectators and entrance to the Grounds and Fête at Rudyard was 6d. Between twenty five and thirty thousand people attended, with many special trains starting from Stoke via Endon and via Congleton and also from Macclesfield. Needless to say, the accommodation at the small country station of Rudyard proved far from satisfactory as the enormous crowds pressed through small gates as their tickets were collected.

Carlos Trower, *"the intrepid high-rope walker"* who appeared under the pseudonym of African Blondin, visited Rudyard again during the last week of June 1878, and performed on three days. The rope was stretched 100 feet above the water, and the width of the lake over which he passed was 200 yards. This attraction proved extremely popular, not only with the visitors from the Potteries but also with those from Macclesfield, with the special trains *"crowded to excess"* and the numbers coming in from Leek were in their thousands. For that week the skating rink was turned into a dancing school, providing the opportunity for many couples to dance.

The coming of the railway in 1850 found Rudyard, Horton and the small population settlement around Harper's Gate still very much a rural community, with farmers, agricultural labourers and domestic servants forming the major part of the local community, together with three publicans, two shoemakers, a quarryman, a wagoner, two wheelwrights, a joiner and a water bailiff. The NSR employed a station master, two labourers and one platelayer at Rudyard. The next forty years was to see substantial property development at Rudyard, but not nearly as substantial as some of the local landowners were hoping. From 1873 onwards, attempts to sell plots of land on Dunwood Lane, Whorrocks Bank (now known as Horton Bank), Lake Road, Reacliffe Road and Lakeside met with only partial success. Some of these plots have only been developed in recent years, and some not at all.

Fox Holes was built in 1856 as an agricultural smallholding and nearby Rudyard Villa in 1860 by Matthew Gaunt, magistrate and landowner. By 1865, Keepers Cottage had been erected in Rudyard Vale, only a few yards in front of Rudyard Villa, and became better known as Spite Hall. A report in the Staffordshire Advertiser in June 1865 provides an explanation for the reason behind this name.

"One particular spot caught the eye of the writer, where there was a new and prettily built and pleasantly situated country residence, occupied by a venerable looking silvery haired old gentleman. But to the writer's surprise, there was a piece of new building right in front of this old gentleman's house in the form of a superior kind of barn, but apparently occupied at one end as a habitation, by a villager. On further enquiry of this barn-looking building, the writer found that it was as much noted in name as the hotel, but not quite so reputably. It was designated by the villagers as Spite Hall. Of course, the writer was more in earnest about the origin of such an unpleasant name. But he was merely told in short words that it was built to spite the old gentleman by a party who owned some land within a few yards of the gentleman's front door. But alas, the quietude is disturbed by this Spite Hall, a standing monument of bitter and unchristian behaviour, a monument when the spiter and the spited will lie motionless in death, and then it will still be remembered and handed down to coming generations and be repeated time after time to the memory of the injurer and the injured."

There are other versions of this tale. Who erected Spite Hall is still not clear after all these years; the silvery haired old gentleman is Matthew Gaunt, and the owner of the nearby land on which Spite Hall was built was William Challoner. That part of Spite Hall nearest the lake remained as a barn until the early 1890's, when it was converted to provide additional residential accommodation for the expanding guest house and catering business of George and Mary Heath, of which more later. Another explanation tells of two warring brothers and a beautiful old tree which blocked the view of the lake from The Villa, the owner of which had the tree felled. The vexed brother then arranged for the construction of Spite Hall to ruin the view from The Villa completely. Spite Hall was also decorated with a series of ugly stone gargoyles pulling out their tongues, which faced towards The Villa. Some of these gargoyles survive and have been incorporated into the rockery in the garden of Spite Hall.

By 1871 Cliffe Park Cottage had been built, as the lodge to Cliffe Park Hall. There was a gap of some years before the next large family house was built. This was at Fair View, on Whorrocks Bank, as the road climbs from Harper's Gate towards Biddulph Moor. The house and lodge were built in 1879/80, by John Munro, who came from Tain, near Inverness, and who established a wine and spirit business together with George Munro, who also hailed from Tain but was not, apparently, a close kinsman. The business was established in the mid 1860s, with two branches, one in Hanley, the other in Bolton; the partnership was dissolved after some years, with John Munro taking the Hanley business and George Munro the Bolton branch.

John Munro, who was a Justice of the Peace for the Borough of Hanley, evidently prospered and, attracted by the charm and seclusion of Rudyard, purchased land and built a large house. This was the first of several investments that John Munro made at Rudyard over the next ten years or so. Firstly he built Tain

Cottage, with a delightful view over the lake and named after the place from which the Munros had originated. In 1888 he purchased from the estate of the late Stephen Goodwin many of the individual plots of land along Reacliffe Road, both for houses and also boathouses along the lake side, which Goodwin had himself purchased in the 1885 auction of the Cliffe Park Estate. This was part of a speculation on Munro's part, in which he was joined from around 1889 by Stephen Chesters-Thompson, a brewer from Manchester, to develop Rudyard as an attractive place to live and play - more of which later.

John Munro took an active part in the affairs of the village, becoming a member of Horton Parish Council and its Chairman in 1897, the year of Queen Victoria's Diamond Jubilee. He died in 1900, at the age of 58 and the lychgate leading to Horton Church was erected in his memory. His son, Murdo Munro, moved into Fair View in 1902, following the death of his mother, and remained there until his own death in 1922. The house and the 18 acre estate was sold on 30 June 1927, along with nine building plots purchased by John Munro from Stephen Goodwin in 1888; four of these were on the opposite side of the road, facing the Lodge, whilst others were on either side of Reacliffe Road; by this time, the plot on the corner of Cliffe Park Road, which ran alongside the lake to Cliffe Park Lodge, had three bungalows on it at a yearly rental of £5.

The first major attempt to develop Harper's Gate (Rudyard) for new Villa Residences was on 21 August 1873, when several large plots of land, leading down on a slope from the Lake Road to the edge of the feeder, were put up for auction. This was to be the first of several, the others being on 2 September 1880, 10 July 1883, 16 October 1890, 16 May 1893 and 2 February 1911. Despite attempts to popularise Rudyard as an attractive location for the well-to-do to maintain their main residence, as opposed to a weekend chalet and boathouse, it is clear that these auctions were not successful in selling off large plots. What these successive auctions - especially that of 1890 - do reveal is that the larger plots were later sub-divided in order to encourage easier sale, and this is confirmed by the date stones on many houses. Why is it that Rudyard was never able to attract people to purchase large plots for Villa Residences? Firstly, those able to afford to do so appeared content to reside in Leek or the Potteries towns, and those who were attracted by the facilities for water sports appear to have chosen the option of purchasing chalets and boathouses with accommodation attached. Secondly, for those who wished to commute to business in the Potteries, it was not until 1896 that a direct service became available for commuters from Rudyard to the Potteries; until then it was necessary to change trains at Leek. Thirdly, the growing success of Rudyard as a tourist destination, with a season extending from Easter to September, no longer offered the serene tranquility sought by would-be purchasers.

Illustrative of the attempts to encourage development was the 1880 auction, with seven plots being offered, ranging from 2,200 to 2,400 square yards, of building land, six of which were on the intended new road, which was to run from Lake Road to where The Knoll was subsequently built in 1894/95. These sites were described as being on an eminence and commanding charming views, and *"all are admirably adapted for the erection of Villa Residences."* In order to encourage purchase of these lots, the catalogue stated that *"It is probable that at no distant period another Lake will be made in the vicinity of these Lots."* - but despite rumours circulating at the time, no such new lake was ever built.

The first two lots at this auction were for two dwelling houses and two cottage houses with smithy and tea shed - as the catalogue said of them, they *"will always command good Tenants and in the hands of energetic persons a large business in the providing of Teas and other Refreshments for the large numbers of visitors to the Lake may be done."* This provides evidence of the growing numbers of visitors to Rudyard and of how local people were beginning to benefit from this.

The following few years saw the building of houses along Lake Road. Rose Cottage (1881), Vine Cottage (1884), Fern Cottage and Underwood (both by 1884), whilst on Dunwood Lane Daisy Bank (c1888 and originally a private school for girls), and Woodfield (c1880). Tain Cottage was built c1883, the first occupant being Henry Cartledge, then tenant of the Hotel Rudyard. Holly Bank, now known as Camrose Hall, was built in 1891 by Hugh Sleigh. It incorporated two shops at road level and offered extensive accommodation facilities. For Rudyard, and Harper's Gate in particular, the occupants started to change the social composition of the local population quite radically, a change which was to accelerate as further residences, but only one Villa, were built between 1890 and 1915. Middle class professional people - for example, an architect, a solicitor, a school mistress and owners of family businesses including a building contractor and a stone merchant, were starting to arrive, which in turn created a greater need for the provision of local services, for example, dressmakers and blacksmiths.

The sale of the Cliffe Park Estate had the most significant effect on the development of the lakeside at Rudyard. After the death of Fanny Bostock on 19 March 1875, London based auctioneers Debenham, Tewson and Farmer, were instructed to sell the 778 acre estate on 28 August 1876, as one lot. In this they failed and nine years later, on 13 August 1885, the estate, now totalling 784 acres, was offered for sale by Debenham, Tewson, Farmer and Bridgewater, this time in 38 lots. The total proceeds of the sale were £31,000, including timber - a figure far below that anticipated by the auctioneer; he referred to the fact that an offer of £49,500 had been refused some years previously and prophesied that *"in the near future there would be such an eruption of Manchester men at Rudyard that property would be enhanced in value."* This prediction was never fulfilled, although over the next century an increasing number of men built and enjoyed boathouses and weekend chalets. The many plots of land suitable for villa residences were sold at this auction, but other than on Whorrocks Bank Road, near Reacliffe Road - and then only in the last 40 years or so - houses were never built on them.

The Reverend Edward Duncan Boothman, who was married to Fanny Bostock's niece, Georgina Bostock, purchased, for the sum of £14,250, Cliffe Park Hall, Barnslee Farm, Birch Trees Farm and interests in around 100 acres of Rudyard lake. Mr G W Stonier purchased the greater part of Reacliffe and parts of Coney Greave and Birch Trees Farm for £4,800. Between Cliffe Park Road and the lake, a large number of small plots of land were auctioned - of a size suitable for chalets or boathouses and conferring upon the purchasers boating and fishing rights. Prominent Leek businessmen purchased plots, including Walker, John Brealey, W S Brough, W Leech, Wm. Tatton and R Challinor. Mr Stephen Goodwin purchased no fewer than eleven building and boathouse plots, for a total of £4,670. Following Stephen Goodwin's death in 1887, some of these were sold on to John Munro in 1888.

The increasing number of excursionists provided the opportunity for many local people to supplement their wages, or the family income. Tea and refreshment rooms began to spring up in existing houses and cottages from 1880 onwards, and were a welcome addition to the facilities provided by the two hotels. The doyen and pioneer of these was Mrs Mary Austin, the youngish widow of an ironstone miner from Ipstones who, from around 1873, rented Spite Hall, then a keeper's cottage with an agricultural smallholding. On 20 January 1892 her daughter, Mary Jane, married George Thomas Heath, who came from a well known local farming family, and they continued to run Spite Hall as a refreshment room with accommodation and in the late 1920's added a caravan park. The Heath family still own Spite Hall, now a private residence, and the caravan park is still there.

As Rudyard's popularity continued to grow, more tea rooms sprung up in the houses and cottages along the road leading from the railway station to to the lake. In 1884 there were four refreshment houses in the village and one which provided lodgings only. By 1888 the tea establishments had increased to six - Mary Austin, Charles Corbishley, George Corbishley, Hannah Goodwin, James Keeling and Harriet Tunnicliffe; there were no refreshment facilities on Dunwood Lane. Some were in the old cottages facing the Station Hotel, whilst others were to be found in the newly built houses on Lake Road. In 1888 a splendid new Dancing Pavilion was opened at the Hotel Rudyard.

When the first boathouses were built at Rudyard is unclear; the 1816 Trent & Mersey Canal Estate Map does not show any boathouses, but the 1844 Deposited Plan for the Churnet Valley Railway shows one boathouse, on the west side of the lake, located within a small bay just to the north of the dam belonging to the Trent & Mersey Canal Company. In the 1875 auction catalogue for the Cliffe Park Estate, there were two boathouses at the south end of the lake. The boathouse nearest to the railway line belonged to the Earl of Macclesfield (it appears on a photograph of 1868), and the one close by Reservoir House belonged to the NSR. The auction catalogue for The Villa, dated 28 July 1885, confirmed that there was a boathouse belonging to The Villa, and following this auction James Nixon, a Rudyard builder, constructed a boathouse adjacent to it. Apart from these two boathouses, by 1890 there had been no boathouse development of any significance at Rudyard

In 1854 Methodist services were transferred to Rudyard Hall, then owned by Mr Robert Needham. This continued until 1892, five years after the death of Mr Needham. During all those years, regular preaching services had been held, but membership remained small - in 1886 there were only three members. Robert Needham's son, Samuel, continued the services during this period. Harper's Gate became the Methodist centre in 1858. In 1861, William Henry Vigrass of Leek, a silk glosser at William Hammersley's Dye Works in Mill Street, became a teacher and manager of the Harper's Gate Sunday School, which was held in a cottage facing the old mill, rented for that purpose. The school began with 21 scholars and religious instruction was provided, in addition to reading, writing and arithmetic. The anniversary of the founding of the Sunday school was a great occasion, extending to two Sundays, with two services on each Sunday. The children were accompanied not only by the organ, but by other instruments including violins and cellos. The Chapel was built in 1862, at a cost of £231, and had seating for 76. Local preachers included J Corbishley of Dunwood. In 1886 membership at Harper's Gate numbered 15, with 36 scholars, most of whom attended the Sunday School in the morning and afternoon; there were seven teachers, three attending in the morning and four in the afternoon. The Minister and local preacher was Mr Enoch Buxton of Reacliffe, Horton, with Class leaders Samuel Needham at Rudyard Hall and S N Haynes and C Rogers at Harper's Gate.

At the turn of the century the annual outing to Belle Vue, Manchester was regarded as a great treat, the pupils travelling by rail. Picnics to Danebridge were also provided, by means of horse drawn wagons, in which seats had been provided.

A 1903 view through the trees of the water bailiff's cottage, built 1851/52, at Rudyard lake. The original water bailiff's cottage, built around the time of the construction of the reservoir in 1799 , became the Hotel Rudyard in 1850 and was enlarged in the 1860s, in 1870, in 1883 and 1906/07, to become the substantial hotel from 1907 onwards.   *George Bowyer collection*

Application by Joseph Tunnicliffe, then water bailiff, 5 July 1850, for a license to sell alcoholic drinks from the water bailiff's house. Members of the Tunnicliffe family were water bailiffs at Dane Feeder and at Rushton for at least 70 years, up to the 1880s.   *Tunnicliffe/Heath collection*

Advertisement in the Macclesfield Courier, 7 June 1851, for the second - and final - Regatta held prior to the 5 year long High Court action which the North Staffordshire Railway lost. Listed are details of the large number of excursion trains from the Potteries, Macclesfield and Congleton, Derby, Burton, Uttoxeter and Leek.

Macclesfield Library

Advertisement from the Macclesfield Courier, advising of the opening of Horton station on 18 August 1850. Whilst many of the local residents wished to see the station opened at the north end of the lake, near Rye Croft Gate, the North Staffordshire Railway could see the commercial advantages of opening a station near Harper's Gate, closer to their intended hotel.   *Macclesfield Library*

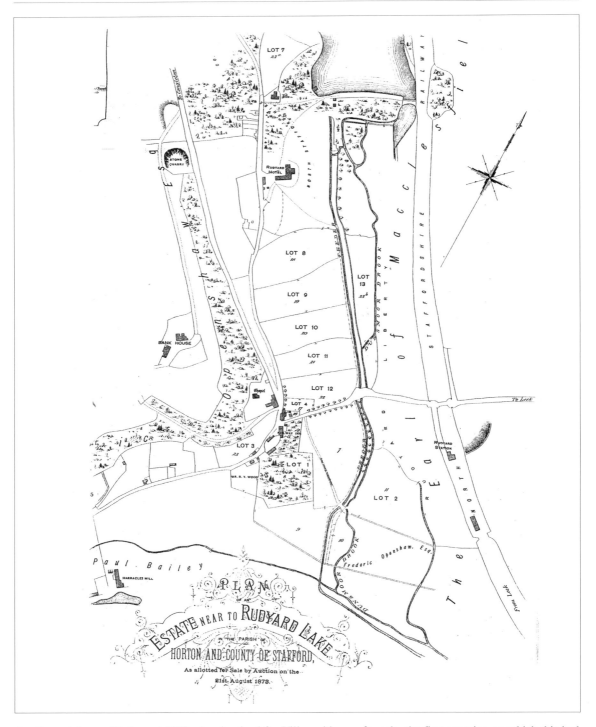

Auction catalogue, 21 August 1873, showing land for Villa residences for sale, the first occasion on which this had occurred. Lots 8-11 are all sizable plots along Lake Road, although none actually overlook the lake.

Author's collection

An advertising card for what is now known as the Hotel Rudyard. Henry Platt took over the tenancy and proceeded to aggressively market both the Hotel and Rudyard, and this illustration shows the extent of the Railway Company's substantial investment in the Hotel. Henry Platt was landlord from 1870 until 1875. *William Salt Library*

HENRY PLATT,
RUDYARD LAKE HOTEL.

H. P. respectfully thanks the public for their patronage since he has been at the above Hotel, and during the short time he would inform them that he has added very considerably to the attractions of the grounds. Parties, either large or small, will find ample accommodation; two days' notice is, however, required when the party numbers over twenty persons.

HOT DINNERS EVERY SUNDAY AT 1-30.

Beds and first-class accommodation at commercial charges. The Hotel offers to commercial gentlemen spending their week end in the neighbourhood the comforts of a home amidst the most beautiful scenery.

TARIFF.

Port or Sherry	4d.
Brandy, Pale or Brown...	6d.
Whiskey, Scotch or Irish	4d.
Gin or Rum	3d.
Ale, Porter, or Bitter Beer	2d.
	Per Bottle.
Port	6s.
Sherry	5s.
Claret and Hock...	2s. to 5s.
Champagne	7s. to 10s.
Bitter, in Bottles...	5d.
Bottled Stout	4d.
Cigars	from 3d. to 6d.
Tea, with Beef and Ham, downstairs ..	1s. 6d.
„ with Beef, Ham, &c., upstairs ...	2s. 6d.
Dinner or Lunc	2s. 0d.

Good Stabling and Accommodation for Horses and Conveyances.—On Holidays Bands play at intervals, and Dancing space is provided if the weather proves unfavourable, the large ball room is thrown open for that purpose.

1874 Tariff for the Rudyard Lake Hotel.
William Salt Library

NOTICE.
RAILWAY ARRANGEMENTS,
JUNE, 1874.

. Visitors are respectfully requested to enquire if there be any alterations made in the subjoined lists. As a rule the Summer Trains continue to run at the same times throughout the summer months.

STOKE TO AND FROM RUDYARD.

	a. m.	p. m.	p. m.
STOKE	11 15	2 35	7 50
BUCKNALL	11 23	2 43	7 58
LEEK...	11 53	3 13	8 28
RUDYARD... ...	12 44	3 20	8 35

	a. m.	a. m.	p. m.
RUDYARD		3 50	8 45
LEEK...		4 0	8 50
BUCKNALL		4 30	9 19
STOKE		4 39	9 28

Special Trains run every Monday, Thursday, and Saturday from Stoke, taking up passengers at Bucknall, Milton, &c., leaving Stoke at 2·35 p.m., and returning from Rudyard at 8·45 p.m.

MANCHESTER TO RUDYARD.

	a. m.	a. m.	p. m.	p. m.
MANCHESTER ...	5 50	9 50	2 30	5 10
STOCKPORT ...	6 5	10 2	2 43	5 25
MACCLESFIELD ...	7 5	10 28	3 28	5 52
RUDYARD... ...	8 3	10 54	4 0	6 24

Trains leave Rudyard for Macclesfield, Manchester, and the North : 8·21, 10·4, 12·44, 6·22, and 8·21.

June 1874 Railway excursion arrangements from Stoke and Manchester to Rudyard. *William Salt Library*

GREAT ATTRACTION.

Rudyard SKATING RINK

WILL BE

OPENED ON THURSDAY NEXT, JUNE 1st,
AT 2·30 P.M.

By the kind permision of Captain E. WORTHINGTON, the BAND of the 28th Staffordshire Rifle Volunteers will be in attendance on June 1st & 3rd.

Plimpton's Patent Roller Skates, for which the Proprietor holds the sole concession for this district, will be used at this Rink.

Open to Ladies and Gentlemen Daily (Sundays Excepted) :

Morning ....from 11a.m. to 1 p.m.	
Afternoon .... .from 2·30 p.m. to 5 p.m.	
Evening ....from 6 p.m. to 8 30 p.m.	

Terms :	£	s	d
Admission	0	1	0
Children under Twelve	0	0	6
Hire of Skates........................ ...	0	0	6
Books of 25 1s admission tickets...	1	1	0
Books of 25 skate tickets............	0	10	6

Pass, admitting at all times (emergencies excepted) :

Quarterly single admission	1	5	0
Including use of skates..............	1	12	0

Subscribers' Tickets will be available for Admission at the Newcastle and Hanley Rinks.

For train service and cheap rates, see Company's Bills for June.

JOSEPH THORNLEY,
Proprietor.

Tickets and all information may be had from Mr. CHAS. BARKER, Sunderland-st, Macclesfield.

An advertisement which appeared in the Macclesfield Courier, 27 May 1876, for the new roller skating rink at Rudyard. The success of the rink depended heavily upon visitors coming by rail from Macclesfield, Leek and further afield.   *Macclesfield Library*

GRAND AQUATIC ENTERTAINMENT,
AT
RUDYARD LAKE,
MONDAY, JUNE 25th, 1877.

CAPTAIN WEBB
HAS THE HONOUR TO ANNOUNCE THAT HIS FIRST GRAND

AQUATIC FETE
WILL TAKE PLACE ON THE ABOVE DATE.

The Programme will embrace the following :—

ALL ENGLAND SWIMMING CONTEST,
First Prize, £5.   Second Prize, £3.   Third Prize, £1.   Distance, Half-a-Mile.

ALSO, AMATEUR COMPETITION !
First Prize, Silver Cup, value £5.   Second Prize, Gold Medal.   Third Prize, Silver Medal.   Distance, Quarter of a Mile.

YOUTHS' SWIMMING RACE
Open to all under 16 years of age.   First Prize, a Gold Medal.   Second Prize, Silver Medal.   Third Prize, Badge.

The Talented Beckwith Family, viz:—

PROFESSOR BECKWITH,
MISS AGNES BECKWITH,
(The Champion Lady Swimmer of the World.)

MASTER WILLIE BECKWITH
Will Perform their Unique Feats of Natation.

MAN AND DOG SWIMMING RACE.
Rescue from Drowning exemplified, by Two Talented Swimmers!

COMIC PART.—The Greasy Pole and Live Pig, also Duck Hunt.
For which Prizes are given.

CAPTAIN WEBB
Will give a Representation in miniature of the Channel Feat, &c., &c.

A GRAND STAND will be erected to accommodate Several Hundred Spectators.

Captain Webb, who swam the Channel in 1875, was one of many participants in the first Grand Aquatic Fête at Rudyard on 25 June 1877.
          Author's collection

John Munro, wine&spirit dealer, originally from Tain, in the Scottish Highlands, built Fairview in 1879/80 and subsequently purchased from the executors of Stephen Goodwin many plots of land on Whorrocks Bank Road, Reacliffe Road and Cliffe Park Road.   *Leek Post and Times*

Fairview c1896   *Author's collection*

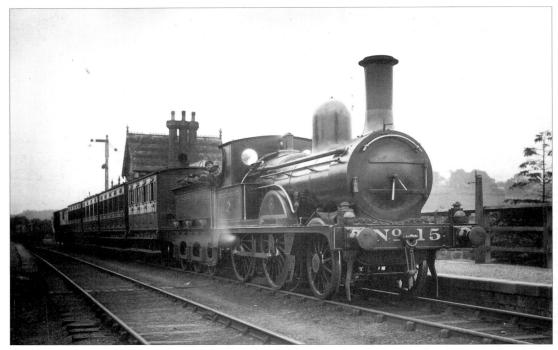

Possibly the earliest known photograph of Rudyard station, probably taken in the 1880s, with a North Staffordshire Railway 2-4-2 C class locomotive at the head of some 4-wheel and 6-wheel rolling stock, forming an excursion train from Stoke.   *Author's collection*

Summer Railway Excursion notice for Stoke Wakes, 9 August 1893
Author's collection

The sale of land in the 1880 auction led to the construction of Vine Cottage in 1884 and Rose Cottage in 1881.
Author's collection

One of the more substantial buildings on Lake Road was "Underwood", with the original construction on the left dating back to the 18th century.   *George Bowyer collection*

VIEW OF RUDYARD VILLA

Auction of Rudyard Villa, 30 July 1885, with a artist's impression of the adjacent Spite Hall, showing it to appear much smaller than it is in reality.   *Author's collection*

An 1885 view of Rudyard Vale with Rudyard Villa (left) and its well laid out gardens. Centre is Spite Hall, with its large field and adjacent plots of land, later to be occupied by a refreshment room and St Elmo's, a weekend bungalow. At this time Spite Hall still had stables and a large hay loft in the section nearest to the lake, but by 1900 two successive conversions provided more accommodation for holidaymakers. Bottom left is the agricultural smallholding of Foxholes.   *George Bowyer collection*

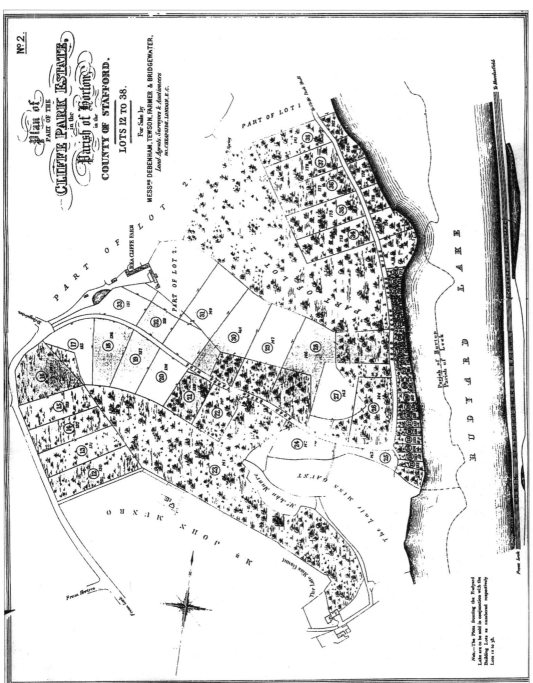

Extract from the auction catalogue of 13 August 1885, showing the sub-division of the Cliffe Park estate into building plots for villa residences, for weekend chalets and for boathouses. The breaking up of the estate in this manner determined the pattern of land ownership and usage down to the present day.

Christine Chester collection

Reverend Edward Duncan Boothman, Rector of Shelton, married into the Bostock family. He purchased Cliffe Park Hall and the neighbouring Barnslee Farm in August 1885, from the executors of Fanny Bostock, who died in 1875.

Christine Chester collection

Below: The Dam in the late 1880s, with the lake on the left and the stables in the background. By 1890, the stables had been replaced by a white wooden fence. This photograph was taken by Sandeman & Hodgson, a firm which established in Leek in 1884. *Author's collection*

View through the Hedge Arch 1890, one of many photographs taken by Bullock Bros. of Macclesfield which were later used for postcards.   *Author's collection*

The Dam End, 1890   *Author's collection* •

The Dam in December 1890, as locals take to the ice in a severe winter.   *Gerald Mee collection*

Rudyard Lake.

GREAT

SKATING
CONTEST

WILL TAKE PLACE ON

SATURDAY NEXT, JANUARY 17th, 1891,

To Commence at 2 p.m.

Mr. Gill, at the Rudyard Hotel, will
offer a number of

Suitable Prizes

TO BE COMPETED FOR

By Ladies, Gentlemen, Youths
and Girls.

ALL ENTRIES FREE.

NO CHARGE FOR ADMISSION.

Author's collection

CHAPTER 4
1890-1923

The arrival on the Rudyard scene of Stephen Chesters-Thompson, of the Manchester based Chesters brewing family, owed everything to his existing business connections, through the wine and spirits trade, with John Munro. The latter had purchased the land upon which Horton Lodge was later built, from the executors of Stephen Goodwin on 12 December 1889, together with many other plots, including Foxholes and Lime Tree Cottages. On 30 July 1890 Munro sold the plot adjoining Fair View to Chesters-Thompson for £1667 and Chesters-Thompson proceeded to demolish the smallholdings known as Lime Tree Cottages, which had been there for a considerable period of time.

Stephen Chesters-Thompson had been an active Conservative politician in Manchester for many years, and was also a member of the Board of the Manchester Ship Canal Company. which at that period was still under construction. He was the Parliamentary agent for the Right Hon. Arthur Balfour, the MP for Ardwick, who later became Prime Minister; it was obvious that Chesters-Thompson was well connected. His main residence was in the then fashionable Manchester suburb of Ardwick. When Horton Lodge was completed, in 1890, he used to travel to Rudyard on horseback, for long weekends, riding from Manchester to Macclesfield, where he changed horses before continuing on to Rudyard. Chesters-Thompson also built a large boathouse to house a steam tug. This boathouse was built into the bed of the lake, with a large, entertainments' room at ground level, consisting of a sprung dance floor with gallery above for the musicians, billiards room and a large balcony jutting out over the lake.

Concurrent with his move to Rudyard, Chesters-Thompson arranged for the Chesters Brewery to purchase the Railway Inn, which it retained until 1897; it was during this period that the Inn underwent a major extension and by 1900 was renamed the Station Hotel. In 1892 Chesters-Thompson established the Rudyard Conservative Association and the Rudyard cricket club; he also made donations to Horton Parish Church and to the Wesleyan Chapel.

Chesters-Thompson over-reached himself financially to a considerable extent between 1890 and 1893, partly through the construction of Horton Lodge and also though his investment, and that of the Chesters Brewery, in Clough Hall Park and Gardens at Kidsgrove, which opened on 28 March 1891. This enterprise was in conjunction with his neighbour and business partner, John Munro. As early as November 1893, furniture was being sold in an attempt to pay off personal accumulated debts. On 13 January 1894, Horton Lodge was put up for sale by private treaty, but no buyer was found. The property was auctioned on 24 April 1894, but the reserve price of £6,000 was not attained. It was finally sold on 5 May 1894 to Mr William Anthony Marsden Tellwright of Wolstanton, owner of the Sneyd collieries, for £5,750, a figure well short of the £8,000 for which Chesters-Thompson was hoping and way below his original outlay of £14,000. Chesters-Thompson's sojourn in Rudyard lasted barely three years, but he certainly left his mark upon the village; the impressive Horton Lodge, the attractive boathouse and the enlarged Station Hotel. He died in January 1899, with some of his debts still unpaid.

The period between 1890 and 1910 saw a rapid rise in the number of boathouses on the western side of the lake; these were built on the narrow strips of land fronting the lake which had been sold off in the 1885 auction of the Cliffe Park Estate. Horton Lodge boathouse was built for the Chesters-Thompson family in 1891, apparently to a design which had been prepared some years previously for Mr John Gill, landlord of the Hotel Rudyard.

The boathouse known as the Lady of the Lake, which juts out from a promontory towards the middle of the lake, was built in 1893. Designed by the highly respected architect William Larner Sugden, who was responsible for many of the civic buildings in Leek, this boathouse owes much of its design to Pre-Raphaelite influences, which were very much in vogue at that period. The Lady of the Lake was built for the Davenport family, silk manufacturers from Leek. Between 1894 and 1899, located between the Horton Lodge boathouse and the Lady of the Lake, a third boathouse was built, owned by the Challinor family, to which a second story was added by 1914.

One of the events that has remained in Rudyard legend is the action of the Leek Fire brigade on 11 February 1895, in putting out the fire at the Horton Lodge boathouse - the second fire within two years. The cause of the fire remains a mystery, but it appears that the brigade tackled the fire from land adjacent to the boathouse, after manoeuvring the fire engine down to the lake side; the ground was under heavy snow and, because of the difficulties involved in winching the engine back up onto Reacliffe Road, the decision was taken to haul the engine back across the lake, which had been frozen for almost three months to a depth of two feet. The ice held and firemen and skaters hauled the engine to dry land.

A sequel to the fire occurred on the weekend of 16/17 February, when the Leek Volunteers and their bands, comprising some 64 men, marched the full length of the lake and back, over the frozen surface. This Big Freeze lasted more than three months and beat the previous record, of 1890/91, by a few weeks. By the Christmas of 1894, the ice on the lake was well over a foot thick, and though the surface, for skating purposes, was somewhat rough, the lake became a popular venue. At weekends there were between five and six hundred people gathered on the ice at any one time.

The Jubilee Stone, erected in 1897 to commemorate the Diamond Jubilee of Queen Victoria, stands at the junction of Lake Road and Horton (Whorrocks) Bank. The stone came from the nearby quarry, a few hundred yards up Horton Bank, which was worked by Peter Nixon, a local builder, who was also responsible for the original lettering on the stone. The Jubilee Stone was broken during its transportation from the quarry to its present site on rollers, and a small join is still visible near the top of the monument, where it has been cemented together.

Comparison of the NSR Deposited Plan for November 1903, and the Book of Reference for its Parliamentary Bill in the 1903/04 session, with the 1898 Ordnance Survey map indicate the following privately owned boathouses, from south to north:

1. Rudyard Vale Boathouse owned by Mary Heath, occupied by Mary Jane Heath and
                                                                       Arthur Hugh Shaw
2. Rudyard Vale Boathouse owned by Mary Jane Heath, occupied by William Hall and
                                                                       Arthur Fogg
3. Rudyard Vale Boathouse owned and occupied by William Challenor
4. Rudyard Vale Boathouse owned and occupied by Percy Mottram Cox
5. Rudyard Vale Boathouse owned by William Spooner Brough and Percy Mottram Cox
6. Horton Lodge Boathouse (not described as such) owned and occupied by Ann Tellwright
7. Boathouse owned by Charles Edward and Reginald Challenor, and occupied by
                                                                       Reginald Challenor
8. Lady of the Lake (not described as such) owned and occupied by Eliza, Minnie, Fred and
                                                                       George Davenport.
9. Boathouse and Summer House owned and occupied by Robert Rushton
10. Boathouse owned and occupied by Fred Darlington Wardle
11. Summer House owned and occupied by George Waller Stonier

From this it is clear that the substantial amount of boathouse development occurred between 1899 and 1903, carried out in the main by prominent textile maufacturers from Leek

The evidence submitted by Petitioners opposing the intended development at Rudyard lake by the NSR refer to the then tenant of the Rudyard Hotel (Mrs Harriet Bilton) also being a tenant of a boathouse at the north end of the lake, and she has *"during the last few years largely increased her number of boats on the lake."* The boathouse referred to is the Chalet boathouse, also known as "Bilton's". The 1925 Ordnance Survey shows the two long-standing boathouses at the south end of the lake, two 'new' boathouses belonging to John Hall, five boathouses at Rudyard Vale, the Horton Lodge boathouse, then two boathouses (belonging to Challenor and to Rigby at Sandypoint, before the Lady of the Lake). To the north of Lady of the Lake, there are three Boathouses between it and Cliffe Cottage, and one further boathouse beyond the cottage, the second and third boathouses being the Brackens boathouse and the Chalet boathouse. Early postcards, some of which are postally used and therefore carry a date, confirm the significance of the boathouse development occurring by 1903.

The NSR Parliamentary Bill of 1903/04 met with predictable local opposition, which was considerable. Given that the NSR sought all embracing powers to enlarge Rudyard reservoir and the Dane feeder, to acquire, erect and construct hotels, and to construct, maintain and let for hire steamers, electric launches and sailing and rowing boats to be used on the Rudyard reservoir, there were many local interests that stood to be adversely affected. Those who felt threatened by the NSR proposals banded together to present a petition to to the Parliamentary Committee scrutinising the Bill; they included the Tellwright Trustees, the Munro Trustees and W S Brough, who all owned valuable residences, Mrs Mary Jane Heath, who owned Spite Hall and also operated a boat hire business, John Brealey, a well known land agent and resident of the village and Arthur Shaw, a boathouse tenant.

To all these petitioners, the real objective behind the NSR's seeking to acquire land compulsorily in order to increase the depth of the lake by 18" was not in order to benefit the canal service by the storage of extra water, but firstly to enable the Company to rid itself of the statutory disability under 1856 Bostock v NSR case, secondly to turn Rudyard lake and the adjacent lands into a pleasure resort, thirdly to increase passenger traffic on the line to and from Rudyard and fourthly to vest in the NSR the monopoly of letting out boats for hire. The proposed Bill also envisaged the conversion of Cliffe Park Hall into an hotel. The Petitioners also expressed their anger at the tenant of the NSR-owned Hotel Rudyard, Mrs Harriet Bilton, who had built a boathouse towards the northern end of the lake and had purchased six or seven boats which were let for hire, contrary, as they alleged, to the spirit of the 1856 Bostock v NSR ruling.

John Brealey made many telling points in his evidence in support of the Petition: *"Life would be, to some extent, endangered by the running of launches and hiring out of small boats to trippers. The NSR seeks to acquire compulsorily Reacliffe Wood and other woods. There appears to be no necessity to acquire them unless they are intended for a building speculation or pleasure grounds for the general public, and most probably the latter, as to make such a great undertaking pay it will be necessary for the NSR to carry crowds from Manchester, Macclesfield, the Potteries, Derby and intermediate stations. Rudyard would develop into a kind of Belle Vue at no remote date and get into the hands of public entertainers. There is a considerable quantity of building land situate near Rudyard Lake in the market, which would have been sold years ago had the NSR provided a reasonable service of trains ...."*

The evidence of Arthur Shaw in support of the Petition also makes interesting reading: *"Rudyard Lake is a great holiday resort on Bank Holidays and there is very considerable trespass by the crowds, notwithstanding notices warning trespassers; Reverend Duncan Boothman, until a few years ago, engaged Police Constables and stationed them on Reacliffe Drive at a very considerable distance from any public road or footpath in order to stop trespassing. Spite Hall, which belongs to Mary Jane Heath, would be greatly prejudiced if her boating rights were taken away from her, as she allows her visitors, both day visitors and boarders, the use of her boats."*

The NSR secured an Act of Parliament on 24 June 1904, having made minor concessions to the various petitioners. The Company was then in a position to implement the draft agreements reached with the Reverend Boothman and members of his family (descendants of the Haworth/Bostock family which built Cliffe Park Hall in 1811), to purchase Cliffe Park Hall and the neighbouring 67 acre estate, plus the adjacent Barnslee Farm of 142 acres. It was Cliffe Park Hall and the land surrounding Barnslee Farm that was to provide the Club House and the course for the intended Rudyard Lake Golf Club. Whilst there was no reference to golf in the Act, the Act contained provisions to build, maintain, manage and lease hotels and, in the specific context of the Hall, the NSR contemplated *"the conversion of the property into an hotel or other place of public resort or entertainment."*

Work appears to have commenced shortly after the Act of Parliament was passed, and a report in the Leek Times on 22 April 1905 indicates the work carried out by then.

"The work of increasing the supply of water from Rudyard Lake was commenced by the North Staffordshire Railway Company after obtaining powers under the Act of Parliament in August last year, and when our representative walked round the other day on the invitation of the company's canal engineer, the work was on the highway to completion. In order to take full advantage of the water coming from the Wincle weir and of floods, the company have raised the banks of the feeder 2 to 3 feet for a distance of about three miles, and the embankments of the lake have been raised and strengthened and the storage capacity thus increased from 850 million gallons to to 935 million gallons, or an increase of 85 millions. Near Wolfdale Farm and at the end of the Lake a station has been built, and this will enable passengers to take advantage of the beautiful walk round the lakeside through the Barns Lee and Cliffe Park estates - a walk which has been denied visitors too long, - the company having made a footpath skirting the edge of the Lake and joining the old drive to Cliffe Park. The station is also situate at a convenient place near to the main road between Leek and Macclesfield. At this end of the lake an earth embankment is built beyond the stone wall which has been raised 4 to 5 feet to prevent the water spreading on the land. The walk spoken of from the Rudyard Lake Station to the Hotel Rudyard is about three miles long and there are few walks prettier in the whole country. The company are making a good footpath and at various suitable spots nice seats will be placed. ....

......The idea in the first place was to prevent the boats on the canal being stopped by a shortage of water, and this being accomplished the company will bring in the pleasure part by introducing electric launches, etc., on the Lake, and if there is sufficient demand a service of motors will be run to various places of interest, but this is hardly likely to be included in this summer's programme."

As a consequence of the work of enlarging the dam at Rudyard, an alternative scheme for gathering water, which had been evaluated by the Trent and Mersey Canal Company's engineer, Mr Edward Smith, did not proceed. Since the Canal had suffered from a serous shortage of water in 1897, this had become a cause of grave public concern; Smith reviewed not only the options at Rudyard, but also those at the Bagnall Valley, with a view to fixing a site on that gathering ground for the reservoir immediately above Stanley. The NSR looked at the alternative plans and costs before proceeding with the Rudyard scheme as representing better value for money.

In the spring of 1905 the enlarged lake, described by the NSR as *"The rendezvous of all Anglers"* had been restocked with 30,000 fish. A station at the north end of the Lake had been authorised by NSR Directors "for Cliffe Park" at a cost of £834: although it officially opened on 1 May 1905, passengers were able to alight only on 22 and 24 April - Easter Saturday and Easter Monday repectively. Foreman William Warburton was in charge on a weekly salary of 23 shillings. The facilities provided consisted of general and ladies' waiting rooms, a booking office, and earth closets (toilets) for both sexes on the down platform. An additional waiting room was provided in the spring of 1907. At the south end of the lake, the main Rudyard station had already undergone major improvements a few years earlier; an additional siding had been added for excursionist traffic in 1899, and the platforms were raised and lengthened in 1902. As a result of the new initiatives, an additional "waiting shed" for passengers returning to Leek and Stoke was provided in the spring of 1907.

Whilst the engineering work was being carried out on the lake, the Hotel Rudyard was being substantially enlarged, with an extra floor being added. By Easter 1906, additional pleasure boats arrived for the lake, whilst a floating stage for the proposed electric launch was in the course of construction and paid for by the NSR. Boating rights were leased to John Hall who built his own landing stage at the Dam below Reservoir House and provided vigorous competition to the existing boat business of George and Mary Heath. Whether it was Hall or Heath who had experienced difficulties with the new motor boats is uncertain, but on 30 March 1907 George Heath of Spite Hall announced by way of advertisement that he had *"purchased a new MOTOR BOAT, one which will not break down, and the same will commence to run on Friday, and will run from his Boathouse on Saturday, Sunday and Monday."* (Easter weekend). By the time Whitsuntide had arrived, George Heath was advertising his motor launch "Grace Darling", capable of carrying 30 passengers.

The NSR also built a tea-room on the hill near the small bay, at the south end of the lake, which was also rented out to John Hall, and this opened towards the end of May 1906. Reference is made to the establishment of the Rudyard Lake Rowing Club in August 1907, and of a challenge race on Saturday 24 August with the nationally acclaimed Burton Leander crew. No further information on the Rudyard Club is yet to hand.

But even as the NSR was carrying out its engineering works on the lake in late 1904 and early 1905, three of the landowners fronting the lake on the west side - the Munros, the Tellwrights and the Watts - started to challenge the NSR's legal powers to do so. The Trustees of the Munro estate obtained Counsel's opinion on 18 April 1905 and initiated High Court action by serving a writ on the NSR on 16 June 1905. The essence of the claim was that the NSR had sought to enlarge the lake by forming a wall of loose stones and earth rubbish on land which the NSR did not own and in consequence the NSR were able to increase the depth of the lake, without having acquired any additional land, but at the same time denying the land owners access to the lake. The NSR settled the claim from the Watt's trustees, but the disputes with the other claimants continued, even to the extent of having to remove 20 inches added to the wall; on 20 July 1906 the NSR's General manager, W D Phillipps, admitted that *"owing to a stupid blunder in our 1904 Act, the Company has no power to execute the works necessary to raise the level in the Rudyard Reservoir........."*

The NSR found itself compelled to go back to Parliament to obtain powers, firstly to raise the weir and dam at the southern end of Rudyard Reservoir by up to 2' 6" above the current level, and secondly to acquire such land as delineated in consequence. Still the Munro and Tellwright interests persisted by petitioning the House of Commons, but they eventually realised that if they continued to oppose the Bill, the NSR would have no powers to purchase the required land from them. The NSR finally secured Parliamentary approval on 21 August 1907.

The NSR's original intentions in 1904 were to estabish a Golf Club, of which the Company would retain ownership, at Rudyard lake. The Chairman of the NSR, Mr Tonman Mosley, at its half-yearly meeting in Stoke on 6 February 1906, referred to improvements which had been made at Rudyard Lake, and mentioned that it was the Company's intention to establish a "golf ground", with tea rooms and other facilities, to induce people to go there for holiday purposes. At the time when the NSR were promoting the 1904 Act, available evidence seems to indicate that the NSR intended to demolish Cliffe Park Hall and build a large new Hotel and Club House. Over the next few years, the decline in freight traffic caused by "the greatest depression visible in all local industries' - coal, iron, steel and pottery - and reductions in First Class passengers through greater use of the motor car, led to a curtailment of certain expansion plans. By August 1908, the NSR Directors were driven to state that "they could not let any more money leave their coffers than would be involved in the dividend". Inevitably, the ambitious plans for the demolition of Cliffe Park Hall did not proceed, and only modest conversions to provide locker rooms and changing facilities were implemented.

The early part of the 20th century was, arguably, the golden era for Rudyard Lake, and offered great commercial opportunities for the NSR, since it had recently lost the lucrative excursion traffic to Alton Towers, following the decision of the Earl of Shrewsbury to close the Gardens. The log book maintained by Thomas Brown, station master at Rudyard station from 1903 to 1915, provides substantial information as to just how busy were Rudyard station and the newly built Rudyard Lake station. The numbers visiting Rudyard would be swollen by those walking in from Leek and the nearby villages. The first entry, for Easter 1903, shows that Good Friday visitors to Rudyard numbered 6,283; for Stoke Wakes 1906, between 4-11 August, 12,992 passengers passed through the two stations; 1 April 1907 saw no fewer than 10,221 passengers, with the 2.30pm train from Stoke running in four portions. These were typical numbers for each year, with special events attracting even more passengers; the swimming gala of 27 June 1908 brought 2261 passengers, whilst the Regatta held on 13 September 1913 attracted 3,337 passengers. The busiest day by far in the history of Rudyard station was on 16 June 1913, when a crowd of 20,253 attended a Miner's demonstration; there were 34 special trains running and no fewer than 88 trains were dealt with in total, an astonishing number for what was, in reality, only a small country station. Competition with the NSR was not far away, however, with the commencement of bus services between Stoke and Rudyard.

Rudyard did not escape the Edwardian craze for roller-skating. The American Roller Skating Rink Company, the promoters of the Rudyard rink in 1909, saw their plans supported by the Leek Times on 29 May 1909: *"Is it not the realisation of a need of a new health-giving recreation rather than a passing fancy? When this latest hygienic recreation exercise is partaken of in a well-ventilated hall, situate among agreeable surroundings, the pleasure of a spin of an hour or two on the rollers is considerably enhanced. Rudyard, with its natural beauties, amply fulfils this condition. We feel sure that Rudyard Elite skating rink will meet with all the success it deserves."* Roller skating continued at Rudyard until the beginning of the First World War in 1914, but never resumed after the war ended in November 1918. The rink building was then taken out of use and the Village Institute erected in front of it. For some years it was used as a laundry by the Hotel Rudyard.

A sign of the expansion of population around Harper's Gate and the lake was the recognition that Horton Parish Church was becoming somewhat remote geographically. Sunday evening services started at the house of Francis Salt at Pine Cottage, Harper's Gate on Whit Sunday 1895, and continued every Sunday evening for some years; it could accommodate around 40 and attendances were high, with Miss Munro playing the American harmonium or organ and a choir of six.

The origins of St Gabriel's Church, situated up Whorrocks Bank past the Jubilee Stone and almost opposite the old quarry, rested in the wish of the late Hugh Sleigh, of Leek, to provide additional facilities for worship around Harper's Gate and Rudyard, both some distance from the parish church at Horton. In his will Sleigh left £500 and an acre of land for this purpose. A meeting of local householders was held in July 1902, which led to the appointment of the Rev Bennett Blakeway of Horton as Chairman, with Ernest Bilton as Secretary. Mr John Brealey, architect, submitted designs for a plain building in the Italianate style, with open bell turret and vestry beneath. The contract was awarded to Messrs Heath & Bowyer for £675; the stone was to come from the nearby quarry, the covering to be in red Staffordshire tiles. The total estimated cost was £850. The foundation stone was laid on 25 June 1903, but difficulties in raising funds caused delays; the work of the architect and builder was complete by July 1904, but it was not until May 1905 that the church was solemnly dedicated and even then it was without its organ. The seating accommodated 100 worshippers, with services held each Sunday evening, conducted by the Rev Blakeway. Horton services were in the morning and afternoon. St Gabriel's was a daughter, or mission church, of Horton parish; as such, it was only licensed for Divine Service and had to be served by the incumbent of Horton, who held services on Sunday evenings. The first sexton was Mr Frank Salt, followed by Mr Henry Heath. St Gabriel's only had two vicars, the first being the Reverend Bennett Blakeway, who was succeeded by the Reverend Edwin Wheeldon; both were shared with Horton. The single bell tolled each Sunday, mornings and evenings, to summon the people to church. Unfortunately the church had been built on old quarry tippings and as a result of the foundations crumbling a landslide caused cracks in the masonry. The first evidence of landslip appeared as early as 1917, when, following an inspection, no action was deemed necessary. At a Church Council meeting on 10 September 1928 it was decided to hold an inspection of the tower and the Vicar made a *"very grave report"* to the Church Council on 2 November 1928, stating that the condition of the building had become unsafe; Mr Gibson, a surveyor fom Biddulph, had examined the foundations and expressed the opinion that nothing could be done to save the structure. At this point the Church Council suspended services and the church was never reopened, the final decision to close being taken in July 1929. It had been decided to erect a new building on a more suitable site, although it was not until 25 March 1930 that agreement was reached to advertise the sale of St Gabriel's Chuch, but no interest was forthcoming. The fabric of the building continued to deteriorate and it was finally demolished around 1946.

Some of the salvaged masonry was used for the extension of the Memorial Institute and some in the construction of Wit's End, on Horton Bank.

The expansion of the population and the increasing numbers of Methodists led to a new Wesleyan Chapel being built on Lake Road. The accommodation provided by the little Chapel on the bank had for a long time been considered inadequate, and the new church and school was welcomed by all workers for the Wesleyan Methodist Church in the district. The architect was Mr R T Longden, of Leek, Messrs Bayley and Morris were the builders and Mr P Nixon was in charge of the stonework. The type of stone was the same as that which had been used for the little Church of St Gabriel. The Wesleyan church was constructed entirely of stone throughout, and was built at a cost of £1,000, a special feature being the sliding screen separating the church from the school.

Foundation stones were laid on 25 April 1912; 15 Principal stones and 19 School stones were laid. Tea was served in the pavilion belonging to Mr Guilliard, of the "Limes" café, which adjoined the site. For the next few months, whilst the new chapel was under construction, services were held at the "Limes" café. The new chapel was opened on 24 October 1912, though with some sadness; inevitably there were those who regretted the departure from the old chapel because of its happy associations.

Similarly, the expansion of the village led to an increase in the number of pupils attending Horton Lea school, rising from 67 in 1892 to 95 in 1904. For members of the Horton Church choir, the annual trip to places such as New Brighton, Chester and Llandudno provided the highlight of the year, whilst for those attending the Wesleyan Sunday School it was the annual outing to Alton Towers or Belle Vue.

The skating rink facility ceased to be used after the First World War. There was much support from within Rudyard for the building of a Village Institute as a War Memorial. One of the earliest events organised was a concert, given by the Rudyard Concert Party, known as the "Wasps", in the skating rink. Those involved in providing the entertainment were Mr & Mrs Denis Elkes, Travis Sandeman, Mr & Mrs Joel Winkle, Miss Violet Bailey, Miss Grace Heath, Miss Hines, Miss Nellie Rogers and Mr Len Vickers. The male artists were all ex-soldiers and the concert raised between £50 and £60. The "Wasps" were replaced in 1922 by a concert party known as the "Blue Birds".

After a thorough renovation, the old Rudyard skating rink was turned into a recreation centre for ex-servicemen of Horton and Rudyard, and was formally opened on 5 January 1922 as the Rudyard and District Memorial Institute by Major Nicholson RFA. Horton and Rudyard sent 85 men to the war, of whom four were killed. The scheme to establish the Memorial Institute had its origins in the War Comforts Committee holding entertainments during the war years. The cost was under £1,000, the money raised by dances and concerts, Flag Days and Carol singers. Much of the construction was carried out by local voluntary labour. It was 70 feet long, 40 feet wide and furnished with upholstered tip-up chairs. John Hall was Chairman of the fund-raising committee, the Treasurer was Travis Sandeman and Denis Elkes was Vice-Chairman. The Memorial Institute was enlarged on 12 October 1934, and a porch added on 10 August 1939, to celebrate the coronation of King George V1 and Queen Elizabeth.

The boathouse developments continued, but at a lesser pace after 1910, north of the Horton Lodge boathouse, with Sandypoint being built close to the Lady of the Lake by the Rigby family of Manchester. A further boathouse was built to the north of Cliffe Cottage c1925. Whilst the majority of boathouses were used for their intended purpose, some did gain a bad reputation - *"they had a name for ill-doing and scandal"*.

The period between 1890 and 1925 saw many changes, not least as both existing residents and the new arrivals, mainly living in newly built houses, offered refreshment facilities and accommodation as the number of excursionists continued to rise. Date stones bear witness to this trend - Pine Cottage 1892, Sylvian House 1893, Albury House 1896. The "lean-to's" at the side of Pine Cottage and Albury House were used to provide afternoon teas and places where, from the turn of the century, bicycles could be stored. Immediately facing the entrance to the Rudyard Hotel two pairs of semi-detached were built in 1896, known variously as The Beeches, The Hollies, Woodside and Deva House, and these were rented or owned by people who provided teas and offered accommodation. People who lived there included Madeline Gleaves, Denis Elkes and James and Georgina Coxon. Sunnybank, on Dunwood Lane, was extended with a tea room and a bakery by John James Abberley, who moved in from Cheadle c1902, and established the family business of shoe repairer and also of providing teas, the same businesses that the family had run in Alton and Cheadle for thirty years or more. John Abberley's descendant, William, ran Rudyard Garage for over 30 years, from c1936 to 1971, whilst Fred established, from 1936, a thriving mobile grocery business which survived until the late 1950s, servicing many villages in the Staffordshire Moorlands, the Manifold Valley and Ashbourne.

The first purpose-built café was at Spite Hall c1902, when a new tea room was added to the existing accommodation. This tea room had been enlarged c1894, when Mrs Mary Heath (née Austin) took over her mother's business and converted the outbuildings into guest rooms. The second purpose-built café was the "Limes", built by James Guilliard in 1906, shortly after his marriage to Emily Dawson, who owned tea rooms at 5 Cawdry Buildings, Leek, much frequented by local farmers.

Around the same time, the NSR built a chalet on an elevated promontory overlooking the dam and the bay, and this was rented to John Hall, who had the boat concession at the Dam. During the First World War it was used to entertain wounded troops. The chalet was burnt down c1928.

Mrs Georgina Coxon ("The Missus"), a shrewd business person, established a catering business on the Lake Road at Woodside c1912, (her husband was the butcher at the Hotel Rudyard, and the family moved from Cheddleton into the village c1903), and then built the largest café in Rudyard c1921, where upwards of 250 teas could be catered for at any one time. During the same period the water bailiff, Arthur Brassington, built his own tea rooms adjacent to Reservoir House and next to the coach and car park of the Hotel Rudyard, Tommy and Bertha Stone moved into Rudyard c1922 and opened a shop, which sold patent medicines, cough cures and Rudyard Rock. Tommy Stone kept his shop open till late; on the counter was an old fashioned alarm clock which had long since ceased to function. Next to it stood a sign that read "No Tick Here". From about 1900 onwards, the numbers of refreshment rooms varied between seven and eight, whilst apart from the two hotels, accommodation was also available at Deva House and at Foxholes. Foxholes started as a smallholding and was later enlarged to become a gentleman's residence, and then used as holiday apartments.

Evidence of just how busy Harper's Gate and Rudyard had become was heard in the application by Staffordshire County Council at a Government enquiry held at Leek on 19 October 1922 to close the Dunwood Lane to Rudyard. PC Jackson, the local Rudyard policeman, gave evidence concerning the use of this road by heavy traffic, and commented that there had been as many as 72 charabancs at Rudyard in one day and that as many as 30,000 vehicles had been counted passing through Harper's Gate in one day. Matthew Knowles, a well known butcher of Derby Street, Leek, had opened a shop at Holly Bank (now known as Camrose Hall), facing the Jubilee Stone, by 1908, in order to meet the increasing local demand from the expanding population. He delivered by pony and cart on Tuesdays. On Thursday afternoons he opened his shop and made further deliveries by pony and trap on Friday afternoons.

ALDERMAN S. CHESTERS-THOMPSON, ESQ., J.P.
(From a Photograph by Mr. M. Guttenberg.)

Alderman Stephen Chesters-Thompson was a prominent Conservative politician in the City of Manchester and a Director of the Manchester Ship canal Company. A member of the Chesters Brewing family, through his trade connections with John Munro of Fairview he purchased land from Munro and built Horton Lodge in 1890 and the boathouse in 1891. The Brewery purchased the Railway Hotel, substantially enlarged it and by 1900 it had been renamed the Station Hotel. Although he lived in Rudyard for barely three years, Stephen Chesters-Thompson left a permanent mark on the village.
Christine Pemberton collection

Horton Lodge, shortly after it was built in 1890, with new fencing and the gardens only recently landscaped.
Author's collection

This is a superb photograph, taken at Horton Lodge on 2 July 1892, on the occasion of a visit to Leek by the Rt Hon A J Balfour MP, a Cabinet Minister for many years, and later Prime Minister: to speak in the cause of Charles Bill.

W Allen, Capt. Hyde Smith, W T Govier, J Challinor, Jas Meakin, W D Spanton
Colonel Phillips, Major Duncombe, C K Blagg, T W Twyford, Sir Charles M Welsely Bt, John Brealey, John Challonor, A Standring
R Heath, Mrs Chesters–Thompson, Rt Hon A J Balfour MP, Miss Balfour, Charles Bill MP, E A Worthington, A Ward, Chesters–Thompson
PHV Hammersley, Hon Arthur Stanley, S Chesters–Thompson T H Bishton.

Stephen Chesters-Thompson collection

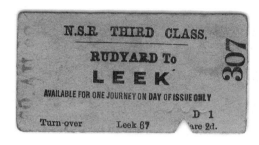

Mrs Mary Austin, seen here at the Dam c1890. She moved from Ipstones to Rudyard c1873 and established a flourishing business at Spite Hall, providing refreshments and accommodation. She passed this business on to her daughter Mary, following Mary's marriage to George Thomas Heath in 1892. *Author's collection*

George and Mary Heath c1895. George was a member of a well known local farming family, who became a local coal merchant and ran a boat hiring business until 1940. Mary, daughter of Mary Austin, inherited her mother's business drive and developed Spite Hall and the grounds as the premier location in the neighbourhood for large events.

Derek Bowcock collection

Above: Spite Hall refreshment rooms c1905, erected by the enterprising Mary Heath to cater for the increasing numbers coming to Rudyard. **Below**: A view of the interior.   *Author's collection*

This Leek Trade Union demonstration, 22 June 1907, on the field outside Spite Hall, was attended by 25,000 people. Trade Unions represented were the Leek Women Worker's Union, the female section of the Braid Worker's Union, the Silk and Cotton Dyer's Union, the Trimming Weaver's Union, the Silk Picker's Union, the Warehousemens' and Clerk's Union, the Silk Twister's Union and the Bakers' and Confectioners' Union.

George Bowyer collection

Following the fire at the Horton Lodge boathouse on 11 February 1895, the Leek Fire Brigade made a return visit to the ice on the following Saturday to pose for this photograph.   *George Bowyer collection*

On the same day, 64 members of the Leek Volunteers, under the leadership of Captain Smith and Lieutenant Davenport, marched to the lake and are seen here on parade on the ice.   *David Salt collection*

A close-up view in June 1897, at the time of Queen Victoria's Diamond Jubilee, of the Harper's Gate cottages. Behind can be seen the newly dressed stone of the enlarged hotel, still called the "Railway Hotel", as the inn sign shows. By 1900 the name had changed to the "Station Hotel", being advertised as both a family and commercial hotel.
Author's collection

Rudyard villagers preparing the Jubilee Bonfire, 22 June 1897
Roger Orme collection

View from the western bank of the lake c1890   *Gerald Mee collection*

The delightful walk along the western side of the lake is captured in this 1903 view of the Cliffe Park road, with the right hand bank sloping down to the lake.   *Author's collection*

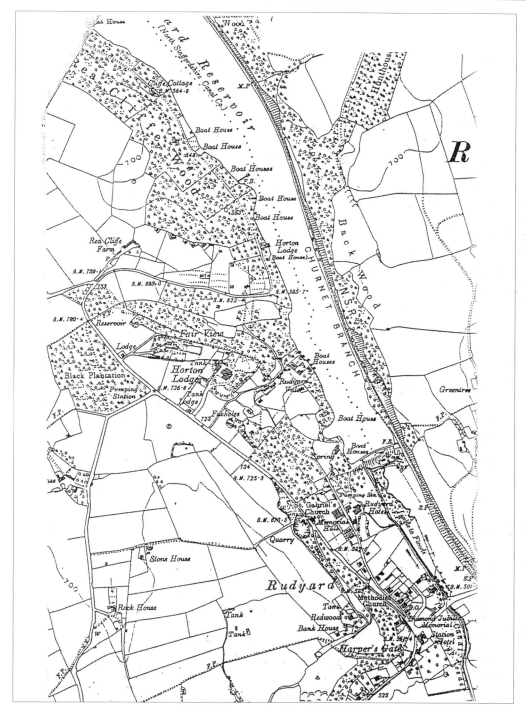

1926 Ordnance Survey map of the southern end of Rudyard Lake, showing the growth of boathouses on the western side.

Courtesy Ordnance Survey

View from the eastern bank c1905, showing five boathouses, each of different design. From left to right they were occupied by; Mary Heath & Arthur Shaw, William Hall & Arthur Fogg, William Challenor, Percy Cox, William Brough & Percy Cox. At the turn of the century it was fashionable for Leek manufacturers and merchants to build boathouses.

George Bowyer collection

Standing on the ice in front of the wooden boathouse c1916 is Arthur Heath and family. On the slope behind is Lake View, one of the many wooden chalets which were used as weekend retreats by industrialists from Manchester and the Potteries.   *Author's collection*

The railway line hugs the shore of the lake in this 1896 photograph. On the far side of the lake stands the Horton Lodge boathouse, (then owned by the Tellwrights), the Challenor's boathouse and then Davenport's boathouse (the Lady of the Lake).
Author's collection

Sandypoint boathouse, just south of the Lady of the Lake, was built c1914 and owned by the Rigby family.
Reginald Rigby collection

Watching the train go by, a 1902 view as an excursion train
passes by the Lady of the Lake.   *Author's collection*

The Lady of the Lake boathouse was designed by the well
known Leek architect, William Larner Sugden, and this is
his sketch which appeared in "The Architect" magazine of
29 December 1893
                Manchester Central Reference Library

"The Lady of the Lake," Rudyard. Real Photo

Postcard showing the figurehead which was
incorporated into the chimney stack of the Lady of
the Lake.   *Geoffrey Fisher collection*

Summerhouse c1908, just north of the Lady of the Lake, owned by Robert Rushton.

George Bowyer collection

Bilton's boathouse c1907. This boathouse was built illegally c1900 and was used by Mrs Harriet Bilton, the then tenant of the Hotel Rudyard, to let out boats for hire, in defiance of the 1856 High Court injunction. Centre background can be seen the Lady of the Lake boathouse.

Alan Winkle collection

These two photographs are typical of the wooden bungalows built in the early part of this century as weekend holiday retreats on Cliffe Park Road, overlooking the lake.
Top: The Brackens, photographed in the 1940s
Left: 1905 view of Bilton's bungalow.

Author's collection

RUDYARD.

M^R. E. BILTON begs to announce a GRAND VOCAL AND INSTRUMENTAL

CONCERT

AT THE

HOTEL RUDYARD, on THURSDAY, MARCH 3rd

(the proceeds of which will be given to the New Church Fund.

ARTISTES :—

Miss LIZZIE WILLIAMS, Miss FIELDING, Miss PHYLLIS BILTON, Mr. J. T. BROOME, Mr. J. H. ADAMS, Mr. W. H. EATON, Mr. E. KENT, and Mr. E. BILTON.

To commence at 7-30.

Tickets, 2/- (reserved) and 1/-, may be had from Mr. Eaton, Derby street, Leek.

Train to Leek and the Potteries at 9-43 p.m.

Advertisement for a concert in March 1904, promoted by Ernest Bilton to raise money for the St Gabriel's Church fund. *Leek Post & Times*

Elizabeth and William Sandeman c1920. William Sandeman came from Scotland and established a photographic business at Ball Haye, Leek, in April 1884, trading as Sandeman and Hodgson. He moved to Rudyard c1896 and was a prolific local photographer and the largest publisher of Rudyard postcards. *Alan Winkle collection*

William Sandeman's house, Greenlands, bearing the datestone 1897, on Dunwood Lane c1905, at what is now known as Sandeman's Corner. The original cottage can be seen in the centre. *Alan Winkle collection*

Dunwood Lane c1900 showing the cottages at Harper's Gate, Rock Cottage, Hawthorn Cottage and Woodlands.
Author's collection

A mid 1920s view of Dunwood Lane in the background, looking towards Harper's Gate. Harracles Mill is in the foreground, whilst far left can be seen Woodlands and Dumpling Cottage.　　*Author's collection*

The two tiny end cottages of the row at Harper's Gate, Dunwood Lane   *Vic Leese collection*

John James Abberley and family seen outside Sunnybank on Dunwood Lane. in 1902, probably just after they had moved to Rudyard. Abberley came from a family of bakers and cobblers based at Alton and Cheadle, and was attracted to Rudyard by new business opportunities. He carried on both businesses until 1912, when he began to concentrate on baking, building a bakery and tea rooms in the grounds of Sunnybank, both of which survived until the mid 1903s. His descendants in the village ran the Rudyard Lake Garage for many years (William), and also a mobile grocery business serving the rural areas (Frederick).   *Abberley family collection*

Looking down to the Station Hotel c1900, only recently renamed from the Railway Hotel. The hotel is seen here facing Dunwood Lane, with the original building, dating back to 1610, framed by the branches of the tree on the right, with the larger higher section being the extension built by the Chesters Brewery of Manchester in the early 1890s. The Post Office was housed in one of cottages on the left. *Author's collection*

The wedding of Syd Hodgskiss and Victoria Harrison, at the Station Hotel c1912. The photograph is taken outside the original ale house at Harper's Gate, being the oldest section of the hotel building. The 1610 datestone can be seen to the right of the left downspout, beside the window lintel. *George Bowyer collection*

Harper's Gate, 1904, looking towards the Station Hotel. On the left is a row of old cottages, including the Post Office, which were demolished c1913 following an accident. On the right is a parade of shops, still looking very similar today. The one known as Rock House, at the far end, used to be an ale house. *Alice Boulton collection*

A view taken from the station bridge, looking towards Harper's Gate c1908. In the foreground, left, can be seen the bridge over the feeder and the steps down to the footpath. In the foreground to the right are the sheds belonging to Messrs Heath and Bowyer, which had in earlier yers been the timber yard of the Earl of Macclesfield's estate.

Author's collection

The only Villa residence built off Lake Road was The Knoll, erected in 1894/95 for John Brealey. This photograph was taken looking south c1905, showing the delightful reflections in the feeder.
George Bowyer collection

Pine Cottage on the Lake Road c1905, was built in 1892, and was used for Sunday evening church services for some years, until St Gabriel's church was opened in 1905. For many years Mrs Hulme provided teas, cycle storage and accommodation for holiday makers. The tea room abuts the house, with an exterior style which blends well with the main building. Note the picnic tables on the left. *George Bowyer collection*

Albury House c1905, a typical family house on Lake Road, built in 1896 and occupied by Francis Salt. Albury House was in use as a tea room for more than 40 years. Notices advertising "Teas" can be seen on the windows of both front rooms, while the sign to the right of the "lean-to", which was used for teas and cycle storage, reads "Every Accommodation for Cyclists". From c1936 until the late 1950s Fred Abberley ran a mobile grocery business from the house. In the background is Sylvian House, built in 1893. *Author's collection*

A postcard view of Lake Road c1905, with The Beeches on the left and the entrance to the Hotel Rudyard on the right. These large houses were used from the outset and over the suceeding years to provide holiday accommodation. and refreshments *Author's collection*

Left: Sketch of the Hotel Rudyard as it appeared on the cover of the Official North Staffordshire Railway Guide Guide 1890. *Author's collection*

Right: Hotel Rudyard in 1905, before the extensive alterations in 1906 and 1907. This photograph shows the ground floor only, beneath the hotel name. *Author's collection*

Hotel Rudyard in 1908, with an additional storey added to improve and extend the available accommodation for visitors. The new stonework is clearly visible beneath the Hotel Rudyard sign. *Alan Winkle collection*

The Bilton family in the grounds of the Lake Hotel c1910. Mrs Harriet Bilton, who managed the hotel from 1898 to 1911, was regarded by many as the brains of the business, whilst her husband, Ernest, from a family of pottery manufacturers, was far more interested in literature. *Bilton family collection*

The Skating Rink opened in 1909 in a newly constructed building facing the Hotel Rudyard. At the time this was a popular craze, with two other rinks opening in Leek at around the same time. *George Bowyer collection*

Rudyard station c1902, looking north towards Rushton and Macclesfield. This is a delightful view of a country station as local farmers wait for the early morning milk train, with milk churns in evidence on both platforms and numerous drays on the left. Most of the milk went to Manchester, but some would also go to London. Despite the growing importance of tourism to the area, farming was still the mainstay of the local community.

Author's collection

1899 North Staffordshire Railway Excursion notice for Rudyard and Rushton. Note the reference to Rudyard Kipling.

Author's collection

Enlargement of a 1905 postcard which shows the full range of station facilities at Rudyard prior to the 1907 expansion of the station. A three-coach is seen departing for Leek. To the right, in front of the newly built goods shed, is a rake of passenger stock, possibly stabled on an Easter excursion.   *George Bowyer collection*

Charles Plant, Rudyard station master from 1915 -1922 until his promotion to Blythe Bridge station.   *Hislop family collection*

NORTH STAFFORDSHIRE RAILWAY.

LEEK WAKES.
On MONDAY, OCTOBER 16th,
A DAY EXCURSION TRAIN for

- LONGSIGHT -
(For BELLE VUE).

Will leave			At	*Fares for Double Journey* 3rd Class Available for return on day of issue only
			a. m.	
Uttoxeter	..	..	8 35	7/8
Rocester..	..	..	8 44	6/6
Denstone	..	..	8 47	6/6
Alton	..	..	8 54	6/-
Oakamoor	..	..	9 0	5/9
Kingsley & Froghall	..	9 8	5/3
Consall	..	..	9 14	5/-
Cheddleton	..	..	9 20	4/9
Leek	..	..	9 28	4/6
Rudyard..	..	..	9 33	4/-
Rushton..	..	..	9 40	3/9
Bosley	..	..	9 45	3/9

Returning from Longsight Station, L. & N. W. Railway, at 10-5 the same evening.

Tickets for this train may be taken in advance For conditions, etc., see handbills.

Railway Offices,   F. A. L. BARNWELL, Stoke, October, 1922.   General Manager.

October 1922 excursion notice to Belle Vue, typical of the many excursions which enabled local people from Horton and Rudyard to travel further afield. *Leek Post and Times*

Rudyard station staff and platelayers c1910, with an extraordinary range of headgear. Note the advertising boards on the right, including Leek Market, Eaton Bros Florists, Salter &Salter for good boots, W W Goldstraw Watchmaker, and A J Salt Ladies' Outfitters. Tom Brown, station master from 1903 to 1915, is on the front row.   *Author's collection*

Rudyard Lake station was officially opened at the north end of the lake on 1 May 1905, as part of the North Staffordshire Railway's exploitation of the commercial opportunities now offered, arising from the new powers obtained by the 1904 Act of Parliament.   *Author's collection*

North end of the lake in 1905, with a view of the back of Rudyard Lake station. There were no opportunities for boat hire here. Note the newly created paths and freshly painted bench. The Dane Feeder comes into the lake where the Dam sweeps round to the left. *George Bowyer collection*

The first Club House of the Rudyard Lake Golf Club at the north end of the lake, which was used from 1906 to 1908, when the Club House was transferred to Cliffe Park Hall. *Author's collection*

A superb view from the middle of the lake, taken by William Nithsdale in the winter of 1905, of a North Staffordshire Railway train passing by en route for the northern end of the lake. Note the different types of craft in the foreground.

George Bowyer collection

Steam boat at the Dam c1905. The water bailiff's boathouse is on the left. *Author's collection*

A typical Edwardian scene c1910 of the Dam, with an enormous throng of excursionists. In the foreground is the landing stage of George Heath's boating business, with his other landing stage accessible from the Dam. The promotion of Rudyard lake since 1905 has by now led to the building of a dance floor, with a shelter and bandstand in the centre of the picture. *Roy Lewis collection*

A wedding party on the boat "Cicely", owned by Geoge Heath, c1910 *George Bowyer collection*

"Grace Darling", seen here when newly purchased by George Heath in the spring of 1907. *Author's collection*

Agostino Granelli's ice cream stall at the Dam c1906. This cart was pulled all the way from Macclesfield to Rudyard and back by horse. Villagers at Rushton and Bosley were able to buy ice creams as the cart passed through.
George Bowyer collection

A delightful view, c1906, of the stall belonging to the Gleaves family at the Dam, with Reservoir House in the background. The Gleaves family moved into Rudyard around 1903, living at The Beeches. This family house provided apartments for holidaymakers, in addition to serving teas and refreshments. The Gleaves moved out of the village c1912.
Author's collection

The Dam c1907, with a lakeside stall awaiting business.   *Roger Orme collection*

John Hall's landing stage c1912, at the Dam. Hall had the boating concession from the North Staffordshire Railway, which built the landing stage and a nearby refreshment chalet and leased them to Hall, who started hiring boats and running motor launch trips around the lake (Adults 4/-, Children 2/-) in the spring of 1906. He remained in business until the start of the Second World War in 1939.   *Alan Winkle collection*

Looking north from the weir at the Dam, a 1905 view taken shortly after the new safety fencing had been erected and painted.
Author's collection

One of the boats available for hire from George Heath, seen here c1910 in front of the Earl of Macclesfield's boathouse.
Roy Lewis collection

A delightful Edwardian scene at the Dam c1910, following its raising and rebuilding in 1906 and 1907. By this time a bandstand and pavilion had been built, and are just visible in the background.   *Alan Winkle collection*

The very primitive landing stage of 1905, used by George Heath at the Dam, on the eastern side of the lake. By 1910 there was a booking shed and a convenient set of steps leading down from the Dam.   *George Bowyer collection*

A scene mid-lake, taken on a regatta day c1918. The boats look heavily overloaded. In the centre, on the lakeside, are three stalls and John Hall's booking office; by the mid 1920s there would be many more stalls. On the far right is one of two boat building and repair sheds belonging to John Hall.

Alice Boulton collection

Chalet at the north end of the lake c1906, facing Barnslee Farm, on the right. Boats and deckchairs were available for hire and the chalet was operated by Mr and Mrs Gale. *George Bowyer collection*

The Lake Pavilion c1908, built by the North Staffordshire Railway and rented to John Hall. The pavilion was located on a promontory overlooking the bay, just north of the Dam. It was burnt down in the late 1920s.
Author's collection

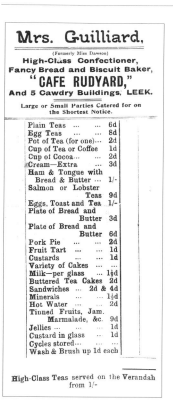

The Limes Café was the first purpose built café in Rudyard and was originally known as the "Café Rudyard", as this early menu shows. The photograph of James and Emily Guilliard was taken in 1906, with baby Frederick on the knee of his governess. *Guillard family collection*

A typical Edwardian tea party outside the Limes tearoom.   *Fred Guillard collection*

S. GABRIEL'S CHURCH,
HARPUR'S GATE, RUDYARD.

DEDICATION SERVICE
On THURSDAY NEXT, May 11th,
At 3-30 p.m. by
THE VEN. J. HERBERT CRUMP, M.A.,
Archdeacon of Stoke-on-Trent and
Prebendary of Lichfield.

An Offertory will be made to defray the
debt and to provide an Organ.

Tea provided after the service at the Hotel
Rudyard. Tickets 1/- each.

Trains from Leek to Rudyard at 1-22, 3-4,
and 4-39 p.m.

Leek Post and Times 1905

RUDYARD
WESLEYAN CHAPEL.

THE
CLOSING SERVICES

WILL BE CONDUCTED ON
Easter Sunday, Apr. 7th.
BY THE
Rev. Arthur Bourne
(Superintendent of the Circuit.)

AFTERNOON 2-30; -:- EVENING 6-30.

Collections in aid of New Chapel.

SERVICES
Will afterwards be held at the usual time in
MR. GUILLIARD'S PAVILION
Until the Opening of the New Chapel.

FRED HILL & CO., PRINTERS, LEEK.

St Gabriel's Church in the spring of 1905, a delightful view taken shortly after its construction. The clean and newly dressed stone and boundary wall can be clearly seen. The driveway in the foreground is from Redwood, owned by the family of the late Hugh Sleigh, who financed the building of the church. Later a porch was added at the rear of the church. Whorrocks Bank Road (Horton Bank) runs from left to right of the picture. The church was built on poor foundations and services were held there only until November 1928. The building was demolished in c1946. *George Bowyer collection*

The laying of the Memorial Stones at the new Wesleyan Chapel on 25 April 1912. In the foreground are young boys in their boaters and young girls in their best bonnets, waiting to lay the stones which bear their own names or initials. *Author's collection*

The Wesleyan Chapel on Lake Road, seen here in October 1912, the month of its opening. *Author's collection*

Skating on the lake c1910. Exceptionally cold winters occurred more frequently than they do in present times. Two photographs where one can almost feel the cold. *Author's collection*

Alan Winkle collection

The Wasps Concert Party, 22 January 1920, was performed to raise funds for the Memorial Institute.
Front Row, L to R; Mrs Peggy Elkes, Miss Violet Bailey, Miss Grace Heath, Miss Hine, Miss Mary Sandeman, Miss Nellie Rogers.
Back Row, L to R; Travis Sandeman, Dennis Elkes, Joel Winkle, Len Vickers.   *Alan Winkle collection*

The next concert party, with some new faces, was "The Blue Birds", again raising money for the Memorial Institute, seen here in 1921 at the Rudyard Tennis Club.
From L to R; Miss Alice Knowles, Bert Brown, Miss Nellie Rogers, Mrs Peggy Elkes, Travis Sandeman, Miss Blanche Salt, Mrs Wood, Len Vickers, Miss Dora Heath, Hildred Salt.   *Author's collection*

Rudyard's football team in front of the Hotel Rudyard in 1922. *Alice Boulton collection*

Rudyard Ladies' Football Team in 1922.
Back row, l to r: Flossie Neil, Ena Fryer, Jimmy Goodwin, Nellie Rogers, PC Richard Jackson, Blanche Salt, Louie Tomson. Eddie Birket, Ella Hall.
Front row: Ada Ball, Hilda Shaw, Elsie Shaw, Bessie Shaw, Gladys Tomson. *Derek Bowcock collection*

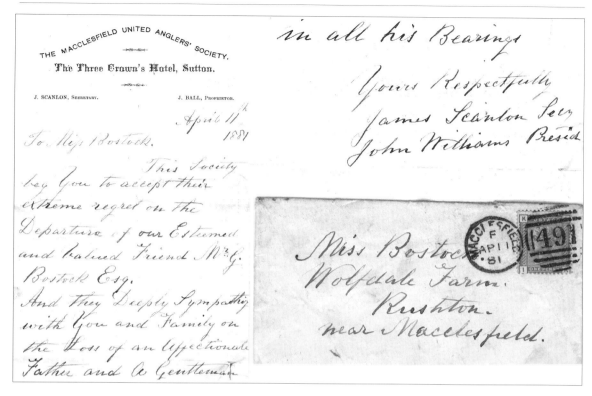

Correspondence from the Macclesfield United Anglers' Society, April 1881.
Christine Chester collection

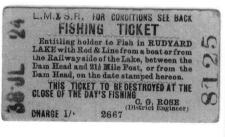

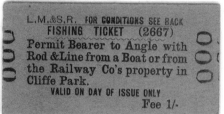

Fishing Tickets   *Author's collection*

Receipt from George Bostock for the fishing and shooting rights let to the Macclesfield United Anglers' Society.
Christine Chester collection

The Jubilee Stone, seen here in the mid-1920s, was erected on 22 June 1897 to commemorate the Diamond Jubilee of Queen Victoria. The stone came from the nearby quarry on Whorrocks Bank. During transportation to its present site the stone was damaged and a section broke off. The stone building centre right was the "new" Post Office used after the demolition of the original one at Harper's Gate, and bears signs "Cycles stored here" and "Teas, Hot Water". The wooden shed in the right foreground was a cobbler's shop owned for many years by Fred Corden. By this time an increasing number were visiting Rudyard by motor bike.   *Author's collection*

A closer view of the Post Office c1925, which faces away from Lake Road.   *George Bowyer collection*

CHAPTER 5
1924-1945

The changing face of Rudyard in the 1920's is well illustrated by the change of use of Horton Lodge. From being a gentlemen's residence, built at vast expense in 1890, for the Chesters-Thompson family and subsequently owned by the Tellwrights, the property was purchased from the Tellwrights in September 1924 by the North Staffordshire Collieries Owners' Association. It was managed by the North Staffordshire Miners Welfare Fund as a convalescent home, where local miners who were suffering from work related illness could stay for a period of recuperation. It was an idyllic setting and, whilst convalescents did not participate in village life, in kind weather they could enjoy tennis and bowls and go rowing and fishing on the lake, with access to one of the boathouses. The Superintendent of the Home, from its inception in May 1925 until its closure in 1948, was Mr John Cooper, with his wife, Minnie, as Matron.

Mr Cooper had been a Miner's Agent (a trade union official) for some years. There was accommodation for 42 residents, who resided for a period of three weeks. The Home employed a gardener (Bill Massey), a handyman (Alf Spode), a cook (Gertrude Spode, then May Cooper, then Peggy Cooper), and several nurses. The Home closed from the end of November until the beginning of February. Whilst there was some initial resentment in the village at the opening of the Miners' Home, this soon evaporated and the locals, such as the Winkle family, put on concerts for the convalescents. Visitors were allowed at weekends, wih no restrictions on visiting times. It is clear that the Home was very much a family affair.

At the north end of the lake, beyond Barnslee farm, about eight wooden chalets were built for weekend use in the early 1920s. Whilst some have been demolished in recent years, several still survive. One, nearest the dam at the north end of the lake, is now a fishing hut known as Oak Lodge.

The Rudyard Lake Golf Club, established with such a flourish in 1906, had a short life of only 20 years, its decline beginning with the onset of the First World War in 1914. The Golf Club had its own Official Handbook, which described the course as the prettiest inland course in the country and went on to say that *"the universal appeal is manifest, since every type of player can enjoy his round at Rudyard. It is brisk, strenuous golf, without an atom of sameness or tameness, worthy of the steel - or rather, iron and brass - of the doughty 'plus', whilst the long-handicap man, though he may perhaps come in with a score as long as a fiddle, will have to admit that he has enjoyed his round."*

The course, enlarged from a 9-hole to an 18-hole in 1908, was short by modern-day standards - 5,119 yards, par 74. The longest hole, the 5th, was 540 yards, and there were six holes that were under 200 yards, with the 13th being the shortest at 132 yards. All the holes were named, some bearing the names of local houses, (e.g. Barnslee, Wolfdale), and others of local landmarks such as Shuttlingslow and Cloud End. The course had excellent greens, composed of fine, springy turf. The lower holes were always in first class condition, being unaffected by the dryness of the summer. Ladies played from shortened tees at certain holes with a par of 66.

Cliffe Park Hall, the Club House - "The Dormy House" as the Guide Book describes it, had a commanding position overlooking the course and lake. Its accommodation included extensive dining, drawing and billiard rooms, as well as spacious bedrooms for those wishing to stay. The 1922 Official Guide advised that the Annual Subscription was £4.4s. for Gentlemen and £2.2s for Ladies. The entrance fees were £3.3s. for Gentlemen and for Ladies, £1.1s. From its early years, when the Rudyard Lake Golf Club was arguably one of the most fashionable golf clubs in North Staffordshire, its decline was rapid - all the more surprising as the course was set in such delightful surroundings. It closed in the spring of 1926, due both to its inaccessibility and the growing competition from other clubs. The ending of the First World War led to an increase, both nationally and locally, in the numbers playing golf, but the Rudyard

Club saw its numbers decline from 230 in 1915 to 100 in 1919, the War and the reduction in rail services being, no doubt, the main factors. After the War, with the growing commercialisation of Rudyard, some of the wealthy families occupying the large villa residences - the Tellwrights at Horton Lodge, the Munros from Fair View and the Johnsons from The Knoll - felt that Rudyard had lost its reclusive charm and exclusivity and moved away. All had been active in the Golf Club and resigned.

After the closure of the Golf Club, Cliffe Park Hall was let, from 1926 to 1933 to a family called Leigh. From then until 1969 the Hall was leased, first by the London, Midland and Scottish Railway Company, and then by British Railways, to the Youth Hostels Association. It was only in 1969 that the Hall passed back into private ownership and it was as late as 1976 that Cliff Park Lodge was also sold out of railway ownership. In 1937 the Hall, as a Youth Hostel, was open all the year round and could accommodate 46 men and boys and 20 women and girls; sleeping bags could be hired for 4d and bathing in the lake was advertised. The hostel was managed at that time by Mr and Mrs A Percival.

Following the absorption of the North Staffordshire Railway into the London Midland & Scottish Railway on 1 July 1923, this new Railway Company assessed its need to retain certain land holdings at Rudyard. On 25 August 1927 various parcels of land were sold - the Rudyard Hotel to Mrs Taylor for £6,350, land alongside the feeder in front of The Knoll to Tom Brookes, and other land to Mrs Brassington, Mrs Heath, the Misses Heath and Mr Robinson and Mr Sleigh; all this represented a considerable disinvestment by the LMS of its Rudyard land holdings. Tom Brookes built Rudyard Garage and the adjacent houses in 1929, but by 1936 the garage had passed to Bill Abberley, in whose ownership it remained until 1971.

The 1920s and 1930s were certainly a golden era for Rudyard. Railway excursions continued from Lancashire, the Potteries and the Midlands; local coaches, including coach operators from Leek such as Gee's, Ferns, Magniers and Weavers, brought further excursionists. *"You couldn't cross the road for charabancs, one after the other. It was tremendously busy in those days.,"* was one reaction, but all this increased activity did, in consequence, drive some long-standing residents away - *"at the weekend, bus loads of rowdy trippers used to come, and mother found it rather noisy."*

All this activity brought in trade for local people, although the competition was "cut throat". Woodside Café was very attractive, and with its delightful gardens had a certain style; not merely serving the passing trade, it attracted church parties, choirs, and was particularly popular with people from Manchester and Liverpool. Many of the smaller houses and cottages provided storage for bicycles at the rate of 3d for so long, 6d for the entire day, and the gardens were full of cycles, as many cycling clubs were attracted. "Brasso's" café, located adjacent to the car park of the Hotel Rudyard, at the top of the bank leading to the Dam, was more modest, with the catering being carried out at the nearby Yew Tree Cottage, with the nearby field crowded with cycles, and later, with cars.

The Dam was a hive of activity. Apart from the boat trips offered by John Hall and George Heath, stallholders included the Sandemans, Alice Winkle, the Guilliards and Harry Breaks, all selling fancy goods; Joel Winkle ran slot machines, whilst Mrs Smith sold tea and sweets. Ice cream stalls included Granelli (from Macclesfield), Podesta (from Leek), Eldorado (from Manchester) and Peacock.

William Sandeman, a Scotsman who established his business at Ball Haye in Leek in April 1884, and moved to Rudyard in 1896, was a studio and commercial photographer of some distinction and became a prolific publisher of the commercial postcards which were very much in fashion from the turn of the century until the outbreak of the First World War.

At the side of the Dam nearest to the railway line, the Brookes family from Willgate Farm had an ice cream kiosk, the only stall on that side. On the Dam itself it was Harry Breaks who became the driving force. Originally from Nottingham, he ran a "Penny Bazaar" in Leek before turning his attention to Rudyard. He was "one of those men who could make money effortlessly". He took over the outside dance floor at the Dam, which had been laid c1907/8, and organised summer dances at weekends and Bank Holidays, which proved very popular. Harry Breaks used gramophone records, with a petrol compressor to provide the power to blow the sound through a horn or stentophone. He would stand on the Dam taking photographs of by-passers and was also a postcard publisher. In the mid 1930s he established an open-air swimming pool at Freshwater, on the Macclesfield road, and this survived until the mid 1960s.

All this activity provided excellent business opportunities for the two hotels. The Station Hotel used to erect a marquee on special occasions, with the Abberleys' having a stand outside the Hotel, whilst on the Hotel Rudyard car park, Kinseys' had a sweet and toffee stall. In the 1930s Alfred Patchett used to take photographs around the vicinity of the Hotel.

Fishing permits, costing 10/6d for the season, were issued at both Rudyard and Cliffe Park stations, and could also be obtained from the water bailiff, Arthur Brassington. The duties of the Rudyard-based bailiff included rising at dawn to walk along the feeder to Ladderedge, where it ran into the Leek Canal, looking for any obstruction. He would then return to Rudyard by way of the 8am train from Leek and take readings at the two towers on the Dam, to record both temperature and the water levels. The water bailiff based at Feeder Cottage, in the Dane Valley, would spend a significant amount of his time walking the feeder, hedge cutting and repairing fences; catering was also available at Feeder Cottage. Whilst swimming in the lake did occur from time to time, it was regarded by local people as a treacherous piece of water and over the years there have been numerous drownings.

The wish of the Rudyard villagers to build a communal hall as a memorial to those who gave their lives in the First World War led to various fund-raising events from 1919 until the Institute opened on 7 January 1922. Typical of these was the concert performance given by ten locals who formed the Rudyard Concert Party, known as "The Wasps". The male members, Messrs Sandeman, Elkes, Winkle and Vickers, were all ex-servicemen. Typical of the Christmas festivities that took place at Rudyard during the 1920s and 1930s was the annual Christmas Party, held at the Memorial Institute on Boxing Day and attended by upwards of 200 children and adults. This was followed by the burlesque pantomime, Cinderella, and then from 9.30pm onwards there was dancing to the delightful sounds of the Rudyard Jazz Band, a group which came, paradoxically, from Macclesfield. At the Wesleyan Church there were performances from the "Messiah". The Travis Sandemans', the Dennis Elkes' and the Joel Winkles' were always at the heart of village activities.

The continuing vitality of Rudyard village was expressed on 20 June 1931, with the opening of a new hard court at Rudyard Tennis club, which had been formed in 1922; its President was Henry Hancock and Dennis Elkes was secretary. The Rudyard & District Women's Institute was established following a meeting on 7 April 1932 at the Memorial Institute. Mrs Harriet Bilton was invited to become President, a position which she held, despite failing health, until her death in 1942. Initially there were 24 members but this had doubled by 1935, stabilising at around 60 at the outbreak of war in 1939. In addition to the regular monthly meetings the Rudyard WI organised concerts, whist drives and fancy dress dances. The funds raised were used to provide the Christmas Party for village children and contributed towards the repair and enlargement of the Memorial Institute. The two highlights of the WI year were the annual coach outing, which over the years included trips to Southport, Blackpool, Llandudno and Shakespeare country, and the annual Birthday Party. From the summer of 1933 and for the next 20 years, the WI campaigned for mains water to be brought to the village, which it finally was in 1953. In 1935 and 1936 they campaigned for the introduction of a 10mph speed limit within the village. During the Second World War the WI were constantly involved in fund raising for the provision of 'comforts' for those on active service. In June 1947 the WI extended an invitation to 20 Polish wives from the Blackshaw Moor camp to attend their meeting. In those early years the WI was regarded as a valuable asset to the village, from both a social and educational standpoint.

July 1932 saw the establishment of the Rudyard Dramatic Society, "which is possessed of an enthusiastic and goodly number of members"; the Chairman of the Society was Charlie Fryer, Jimmy Tomson was Secretary and Denis Elkes was Treasurer. The Society's first production, in November 1932, was of a comedy called "Caste", and money was raised for the Leek Memorial Cottage Hospital and for the Rudyard Institute.

For the villagers, activities centred on the two churches, St Gabriel's Church and the Wesleyan

Chapel, and there was a tennis club, a hockey team and Saturday night whist drives followed by dances, organised over the years by Denis Broster or by Mr and Mrs Moodie, from Leek. Prior to the suspension of services at St Gabriel's Church in 1928, the morning service was held at Horton Church and the evening service at St Gabriel's. The annual big day out for the 16-strong choir was the trip to Rhyl or New Brighton, with each chorister being given 1d for each time he had attended choir.

The Pool End Water Scheme. with its pumping house on the Macclesfield Road, opened on 13 October 1935, pumping an estimated one million gallons per day along a $2^{1}/_{4}$ mile pipeline to Leek, to serve the townsfolk; it was not until 1953 that mains water reached Rudyard.

The Rover Scouts first came to Rudyard in 1936, and occupied Moreton's bungalow on the eastern side of the lake, directly facing the Cliffe Park Cottage, occupied by Mr and Mrs Abraham Robinson. The Rover Scouts were a small group, established by Laurence Fleet, who at that time was Commissioner of the Hanley Division of the Sea Scouts. Over the winter of 1936, the Rovers built the guard boat "Venture", by rebuilding what was thought to be a former lifeboat, but appears very similar to one of the boats operated by John Hall, which was probably nearing the end of its working life as a passenger boat. Sadly, in December 1939, in heavy frost, "Venture" was frozen into the ice and eventually became holed and sank at her moorings. She was raised but never refloated and was used as a bunk-house until c1950, when she finally became so decrepit that she was eventually broken up and burnt.

Between 1939 and 1945, wartime Rudyard saw some changes. Fairly soon after the outbreak of hostilities, in order to prevent German seaplanes from landing, two trip wires were placed across the lake, together with an assortment of old telegraph poles. A pill box was erected on the side of the lake, at the northern end, part of a line of defences stretching from Derby to Manchester and another on the Rudyard Road, approaching the station bridge from the Macclesfield Road. Rudyard had its own Home Guard (as did, for example, the nearby village of Rushton), of about 20 men. For a while, the station bridge was barricaded, to prevent anything from coming through. Holly Bank was the base for the Home Guard, whilst the Air Raid Precautions (ARP) depot was at Mrs Bailey's (the Post Office). During the war Matthew Knowles used his shop as a distribution centre for meat rations; after the war he never reopened, but served his Rudyard customers by van. With petrol rationing in force, Abberley's garage was used by Frank 'Stycco' Ball to make glue for the war effort. At the north end of the lake, the bunkers of the former Golf Course were levelled to help the war effort. Occasional clusters of bombs were dropped on the area.

The spring of 1944 saw the arrival of some members of the American army, who were living in a nearby tented camp on Blackshaw Moor, and came down to Rudyard to test the waterproofing of engines in advance of the D-Day invasion of Northern France in June 1944. Their amphibious landing vehicles, 'Ducks', were driven from the Congleton Road to the north end of the lake, where they were tested.

Tragedy occurred on 27 May 1944, when a Sterling Bomber on a RAF training flight, en route to the Menai Straits, crashed on the west side of the lake, 100 yards to the south of Cliff Park Hall; four of the crew were killed. Sadly, three of the four survivors were killed later in the war.

Between the ending of the war in Europe in May 1945 and the Japanese surrender in August 1945, the Royal Inneskillen Fusiliers came to Rudyard to practice jungle warfare. They had a small tented camp, which was protected by guards. The American commander of the camp at Blackshaw Moor kept a high powered speed boat on the lake for a while.

During the war years, Cliffe Park Hall was tremendously popular as a Youth Hostel; being accessible from both Manchester and the Potteries, it attracted a lot of young people and Rudyard continued to host visitors. The tea rooms remained very busy, despite food rationing. Socially, the village was a hive of activity, with the Saturday night dances at the Memorial Institute bringing in people from Leek and the surrounding villages, as well as the locals, and the Christmas pantomime went ahead as usual. There were some half dozen evacuees in the village, mainly from London. The Miners' Home continued to receive local miners, together with, for a while, evacuees. The winters of 1940 and 1942 were extremely severe, with the lake hard frozen.

The use of Rudyard lake for fishing stretches right back to the original construction of the reservoir.

Those with property rights, through their ownership of the banks, enjoyed fishing themselves, as well as letting out their fishing rights to others. Carp, bream, roach and perch were then plentiful. Early records of use by Angling societies are scanty, but by 1881 the Macclesfield United Anglers Society held exclusive rights for fishing and shooting on the Wolfdale estate, at the northern end of the lake, which it rented from George Bostock for £5 per annum. By 1924, the name had been changed to the Ye Olde Central Angling Society, with membership still drawn mainly from the Macclesfield area, and subsequently to Ye Olde Central Angling Society. Many people fished the lake, not as members of established fishing clubs, but as private individuals, obtaining a daily fishing permit from the Water bailiff.

Advertising postcard for "Freshwater", the open air swimming pool on the Macclesfield road, which Harry Breaks opened in the mid 1930s. It lasted for about 30 years. *Author's collection*

This summertime scene c1966, demonstrates the ongoing success of Freshwater as a popular local attraction. *Mary Bloore collection*

Jim and Georgina Coxon outside Willgate Cottage, one of the Earl of Macclesfield's estate cottages, c1908. Jim was a butcher by trade, moving from Cheddleton to Rudyard, where he worked as a butcher and barman at the Hotel Rudyard. The family moved to Woodside c1912, where Georgina established her successful catering business. All the daughters assisted in the kitchen for many years..

Alice Boulton collection

Woodside Café menu
Author's collection

Woodside Pavilion, Rudyard.

MRS. COXON.

LUNCHEON.

Soup, Fish, Joints, Vegetables, Sweets, Cheese & Biscuits, Pickles.	4/6.
Roast Beef or Lamb, Sauce, Vegetables, Sweets.	2/6.
Cold Beef, Salad, Sweets, Cheese & Biscuits, Coffee.	2/6.
Ham & Eggs, Bread & Butter, Pickles, Sweets.	3/-.

Subject to alteration.
Special quotations for large parties on application.

TEAS.

Brown & White Bread & Butter, Preserves, Cake.	1/3.
Fruit & Cream, Bread & Butter, Cakes.	2/3.
Cold Ham, Salad, Bread & Butter, Sweets.	2/3.
Ham & Tongue, Salad, Bread & Butter, Sweets.	2/6.
Lobster, Salad, Bread & Butter, Fruit & Cream or Trifle, Cakes.	3/6.
Chicken & Ham, Salad, Bread & Butter, Trifle or Fruit & Cream, Cakes.	3/6.
Fresh Salmon, Salad, Mayonaise Sauce, Fruit & Cream or Trifle. Cakes.	3/6.

Woodside Café. Owned by the successful Georgina Coxon, the café originated c1912 at the family home, seen in the background. The business was extended by the building of a wooden pavilion in the early 1920s, making it the largest café in the village, capable of seating upwards of 250 people.   *Alice Boulton collection*

Rudyard Tennis Club c1910. Tennis was a popular recreation, with the courts located in the fields just beyond the railway bridge, on the left hand side of the road when travelling towards Leek.   *George Bowyer collection*

Boxing Day pantomimes at the Memorial Institute were a feature of Rudyard life from the early 1920s until the late 1940s. This is a production of Aladdin, with George Wheeldon on the far left of the picture.
Derek Bowcock collection

Kingswood store 1924, was built by Tommy Brunt on the Lake Road in 1923 for Tommy Stone. Tommy Stone was allegedly a former spy and private secretary to Queen Mary. He held the responsibility for Fist Aid provision within the village until 1955. Prominently advertised is Rudyard Rock, which was only available from the shops and cafés of Rudyard. *Author's collection*

Brassington's café c1930, a view looking north along Lake Road, with the entrance to the Hotel Rudyard car park on the right. Arthur Brassington was a water bailiff for many years; he lived at Reservoir House and, as for many locals, the seasonal income from the café was very important. *Ivan Nixon collection*

Motorbike racing around Rudyard in the mid 1920s - a rare event.   *Alice Boulton collection*

Mr and Mrs Patterson, landlords of the Station Hotel, seen in front of the Pavilion of the Rudyard Bowling Green in the early 1930s.   *Roger Orme collection*

Rudyard Lake Golf Club;
the Dining Room.
Author's collection

Rudyard Lake Golf Club silver spoon awarded as a prize to
a member of the Bilton family in 1909.
Bilton family collection

1922 view from the 10th hole in front of Barnslee Farm, with several bunkers for the unwary. At 448 yards long,
this was the third longest of the course and was called Halfway House. Note the trespassing cows from Barnslee
Farm.
Author's collection

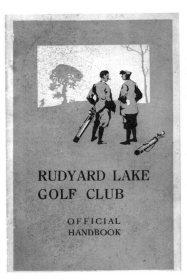

The 17th Green, 'Paradise', which was located just to the south of Cliffe Park Hall All the holes were given names and the idyllic setting of the 17th, which was parallel to the lake certainly justified its given name. It was 266 yards long and was a bogey 4.   *Author's collection*

RUDYARD LAKE
GOLF CLUB

OFFICIAL
HANDBOOK

1922 Handbook, published by Ed J Burrow of Cheltenham.
              Bilton family collection

The first intake of miners at Horton Lodge in May 1925, with Minnie and John Cooper, Matron and Superintendent, seated, front row. Contrast this photograph with the one on page 52 of the 1892 Conservative Party election meeting.   *Cooper family collection*

The Miners' bowling green and tennis courts. Horton Lodge.
Author's collection

Minnie and John Cooper, who managed the Miners' Home at Horton Lodge for the duration of its existence from 1925 to 1948. *George Bowyer collection*

A fine view of the North Staffordshire Miners' Welfare Home at Rudyard - formerly Horton Lodge. John Cooper and Matron Minnie Cooper, his wife, seen here with nursing staff at the side of the Lodge, with its elegant conservatory on the right. *George Bowyer collection*

Shady Oaks, near Spite Hall, was one of several chalets built at the turn of the century by Tommy Brunt, a clockmaker from Congleton, seen here on the right of the photograph; he kept these properties under repair and rented them out.

Below: Another of the wooden chalets located near to Spite Hall, which were built at the turn of the century.

Derek Bowcock collection

The caravan site in front of Spite Hall was developed from the late 1920s by the Heath family, after they had purchased land from the London Midland & Scottish Railway in the auction of 25 August 1927.

Alice Boulton collection

From the turn of the century Rudyard witnessed the erection of bungalows, originally as weekend holiday homes, but in more recent years as main residences. This is a mid-1920s view, looking west across Reacliffe Road.

Author's collection

The popularity of Rudyard Lake is best illustrated by this Harry Breaks postcard from the mid 1920s. There is dancing on the boards with the crowd looking on, people massing around the numerous stalls at the far end of the Dam and several boats about to embark for a cruise around the lake. On the far right are John Hall's boat repairing sheds.
Geoffrey Fisher collection

Fortside, a delightful boathouse built by Bill Burdis in the early 1930's, seen here c1945.   *Burdis family collection*

Awaiting a spin on the dance floor at the Dam are three ladies dressed in the clothes and hats of the 1920s. Note the grass peeping up through the wooden boards.   *Author's collection*

A typical early 1930s excursion train to Rudyard, with a former North Staffordshire Railway 0-6-2T DX class locomotive at Rudyard Lake station, re-named in 1926.   *Author's collection*

One of the last boathouses to be built on the lake, north of the "Lady of the Lake", seen here on the right, c1928.
It later burnt down. *George Bowyer collection*

Members of the Cliffe View Angling Society, who fished at the north end of the lake, seen here in the 1930s.
Ye Olde Central Angling Society

Rover Scouts from Stoke first came to Rudyard in the summer of 1936. Their successors, the Sea Scouts, were established in 1938. They had use of a hut belonging to Mr Moreton. Here they are seen making a last ditch attempt to rescue the rapidly sinking 'Venture'   *Jim Ridgway collection*

The Rudyard Home Guard c1940   *Cooper family collection*

Map drawn in June 1944, depicting the lake during the Second World War. The map shows the location of the wires across the lake, designed to prevent enemy invasion. Also visible, centre, is the camp used by American servicemen from Blackshaw Moor for testing amphibious landing craft. 100 yards south of Cliffe Park Hall is the site of the crash of the RAF bomber.

Christine Chester collection

CHAPTER 6
1946-1997

It was a time of change after the Second World War, as the older generation that had seen the rise and expansion of Rudyard's tourism passed away. Both the Hall and Heath families, who had run the competing boating interests at the south end of the Lake for over 30 years, ceased to trade.

The Maynard brothers, from Leek, acquired various interests at Rudyard. George Maynard took over Hall's boating business and operated some 50/60 rowing boats, employing George Young, the extremely likeable one-armed boat repairer and builder, who had worked for John Hall for some 30 years; amongst the Maynard boats were the "Rudyard Queen" and "Rudyard Princess", both former lifeboats which had been purchased from Birkenhead just after the war. Following the death of George Maynard, his son, Colin, took over the boat business and operated in until around 1969. Over the years, the number of boats he operated gradually declined to 25 or 30 as the costs of repairing them escalated; higher rental charges from British Waterways, coupled with a diminishing number of visitors to Rudyard, eventually put an end to this business and the boating tradition on the lake.

Arthur Maynard, George's brother, had a small café at the bottom of the bank and organised dances at the Dam, where also, for one season, wrestling matches were held, with screens erected around the bank side to prevent anyone from watching without paying. Arthur also operated petrol driven mini-cars or "Dodgems" on the bank. The dancing ceased in the early 1950s, following Arthur's death, but his stalls were taken over by Ted Roberts, together with the hobby-horse roundabouts from Bob Neill. These entertainments continued until around 1966.

A large wooden shed stood on the car park of the Hotel Rudyard, which housed slot machines. This had been operated since the mid-1930s by Fred Horam, a dapper man, originally from Oldham, who during the war resided with the Coopers at the Miners' Home. When he retired in the mid-1950s the business passed to Gordon Rogers, who kept it until his own retirement in the late 1970s. The arcade continued to operate throughout the 1980s but is now gone.

By the early 1950s Rudyard had *"lost its gentility and tranquillity and began to look tatty."* The modernisation of the Hotel Rudyard at that time, with its new banqueting suite, dining rooms and bars, *"brought riff-raff from Manchester and Liverpool; there were fights every Saturday and the Police were called."* Rowdyism on the Dam was creating local concern. Despite this trouble, the Saturday night dances stole clientele away from the dances held at the Memorial Hall. Many of the villagers felt that their village had been ruined, as coachloads of youngsters from as far afield as Derby and Liverpool descended on Rudyard for a night out.

After the war an increasing number of people had motor cars and the numbers visiting Rudyard by bicycle or day excursion declined, leading, in turn, to a reduction in the number of cafés. The once-proud Woodside Café was sold, c1950, to Mr Caldwell, and then to Mr Lorenz, who served fish and chips; it finally closed in 1973 and new houses were built on the site in 1986/87. The "Limes" café was sold by the Guilliard's to the Challoner's in the mid-1930s and continued to operate until the 1970s. The Tennis Club was still active until as late as 1966. The Brassington café, at the top of the bank and adjacent to the water bailiff's house, lasted until the mid-1980s.

The social composition of the village began to alter, partly due to the building of a small number of new houses. On the road leading towards Biddulph Moor there was Wits End (1947), Half Acre (c1955) and Beam End (c1960), which was uncompleted and has only recently (October 1996) been sold in its unfinished state. The Crescent, a cul-de-sac of council houses, was created at the far end of Lake Road in 1955; new houses were built on Lake Road, facing the Hotel Rudyard car park, in 1986 and 1987, with Kingswood, built by Tommy Stone, being demolished during the same period. Fair View ceased to be a private residence c1990 and has become a nursing home. Inevitably, all these changes have brought newcomers into the population of the village, with very few of the old Rudyard families remaining.

For the villagers themselves, the Tennis Club was just about ticking over after the war, but not for long. The once much-vaunted Rudyard Christmas Pantomime lasted until the mid to late 1950s. The WI was still the life blood of the village; prominent members have included Mrs Denis Elkes, Violet Leese, Nellie Sandeman, Mary Brookes and May Brookes, Alice Boulton and Mrs Hudson and Mrs James.

The gradual running down of services on the Churnet Valley railway, (by now in the ownership of British Railways), led to the closure of Cliffe Park station (for many years an unmanned halt) and Rudyard Lake station for passenger traffic on 7 November 1960, which inevitably further reduced the numbers of visitors.

On 16 August 1953 a group of anglers decided to establish a new angling club; they were encouraged to do so by Teddy Chamberlain, who arrived in Rudyard in 1952 as the landlord of the Hotel Rudyard, and whose family ran the pub until 1986. At its initial meeting there were 25 members, drawn equally from Manchester and the Potteries. Various trophies are competed for on an annual basis, but over the years anglers have felt that Rudyard has been neglected. There has, however, in more recent years, been substantial improvement. Since the death of Teddy Chamberlain in 1966 the Hotel Rudyard Angling Club trophy is competed for no longer; the Club is now re-named the Rudyard Angling Club, with 20 members (the limit being 30) and with an annual subscription of £5.

With the building of a new convalescent home in Blackpool, the North Staffordshire Miners Welfare Association vacated Horton Lodge in 1948, and for the next two years it was used by the Workers Education Association for weekend courses, whilst the Wedgwood Memorial Institute was being built. In April 1950, Stoke-on-Trent Education Committee purchased Horton Lodge for use as a special school and on 2 May 1950 it was opened to cater for the needs of delicate and cerebral palsied children. With delightful views over the lake, it was considered an ideal place for children from the city. Initially, 13 delicate children and three suffering from cerebral palsy were cared for, all living in the house. There was a teaching complement of 6/7, with Miss J H Eaton appointed in September 1950.

In October 1954, a new specially designed unit, consisting of a classroom, opened for the young, cerebral palsied children. In the early 1960s there were 30 delicate children and three with cerebral palsy, but over the next few years the composition of the school changed and the numbers of those with cerebral palsy increased. Since 1969 the school has been entirely devoted to the education of children with special needs. Since April 1974 the school had been under the administration of Staffordshire County Council Education Committee with the staff being either County Council or Health Authority employees. The numbers on roll have remained at an average of 30 pupils. From 1969 until July 1996 Mr Roger Orme was the resident headmaster.

The Rudyard Lake Sailing Club started to make an impact on the local scene in the mid-1950s. As a result of an advertisement placed in local newspapers on 15 September 1956, an inaugural meeting was held in one of the lakeside bungalows and attended by a few local 'Heron' owners, who were mostly new to dinghy sailing. From an initial membership of four the club grew. Those attending agreed to purchase Phillip Shenton's lakeside cottage and to form Rudyard Lake Sailing Club; during the winter the building was adapted for use as a club house and sailing commenced in 1957, with eight boats. By the end of the season the fleet had increased to 21 boats and a further piece of land was acquired for berthing purposes. By 1958 the club was still growing and was was able to obtain a lease from the British Transport Commission, now the British Waterways Board, on 1¾ acres of land with a 300 yard lake frontage, and also the lease on a disused building (Cliffe Park Lodge) adjoining the plot, together with ground suitable for car parking purposes.

In the years that followed, the Lodge was adapted to provide small changing rooms and a kitchen, and during 1962/63 a prefabricated wooden building was erected on the site; this was subsequently enlarged in 1978. Membership continued to grow and by 1971 there were 190 members and 121 boats. From around that time onwards, the lack of shore accommodation was becoming a serious handicap and the membership entry had to be restricted, curtailing any further growth until such time as improved facilities could be provided. It is difficult to compare the numbers in membership over the years, because of changes in membership categories, but the size of the boat fleet has dropped from its peak of 121 in 1972 to 70 in 1996. Since 1990 it has been difficult for the club to maintain the membership levels, as the lake started to lose water. Essential remedial work and summers of drought curtailed the opportunities for sailing. When Cliffe Park Lodge was put up for sale in 1976 by the British Railways Property Board (it was part of the Cliffe Park Estate which had been purchased by the North Staffordshire Railway as far back as 1905, and had remained in railway ownership), the Sailing Club failed to purchase it. The property passed into private hands and has remained derelict and unrestored ever since.

The Club attracts membership from a wide catchment area; Staffordshire and the Potteries, Congleton and South Cheshire and South Manchester. Aimed at the whole family, it offers training for beginners and racing for the more competent; the season runs from March to December.

The wider use of Rudyard lake did not come about without difficulties, and British Waterways and the British Transport Commission Police were confronted with the problem of how control could be exercised over boat owners and water skiers who were travelling over the waters at high speeds and thereby disturbing other users of the lake, and also causing erosion problems to the banks. British Waterways were faced with the difficulty that there was no specific bye-law which prohibited speeding or water skiing. A successful prosecution in December 1961 related to the failure to obey the lawful orders of the Reservoir attendant, Ivan Nixon. The conclusions of a British Waterways meeting held in December 1961 were that Railway Police, in a boat supplied by the British Waterways Board, should police the lake during busy periods, i.e. Saturdays and Sundays, and warn those who came to water ski; it was thought that the presence of uniformed police officers would act as a deterrent and prevent misconduct by the drivers of speed boats. The outcome was that Ivan Nixon was provided with a boat to patrol the lake, and he was reinforced by two British Transport Commission Police every Sunday. New Notices were posted, advising the public of British Transport Commission Canal Bye-laws. The maximum penalty for breach was £5.

The greatest threat to the property around the lake came in early 1970 from the Mersey and Weaver River Authority with its proposal to significantly raise the level of the reservoir dam in order to capture and contain more water. This was to be a massive scheme, with costs escalating from an initial estimate of £2.7 million to £6 million. The main line of the Dam would move northwards to the Hotel Rudyard, which would have the effect of flooding not only all the boathouses, but also all houses situated to the north of the Chapel, along Lake Road. It was also proposed that replacement houses be built on Whorrocks Bank. Opposition from both Horton and Rushton Parish Councils, together with the specially formed Dane Valley & Rudyard Lake Protection Committee, mobilised local opposition. In the summer of 1971 the River Authority's Statement of Policy indicated that if the Brenig scheme in Wales was promoted and constructed, it would not be necessary to pursue the Rudyard scheme before 1981. The Parish Council pressed for the scheme to be removed from the list.

Steam railways did not return to the shores of Rudyard lake until June 1978, with the arrival of a $10^{1/4}$" inch gauge railway, owned and operated by Brian Nicholson, at that time headmaster of Waterhouses Secondary school. A line of track was laid at Rudyard and the train ran for about two years. There then followed an interval until 1983, when Mr Peter Hanton of Congleton sought and obtained planning approval to run a $10^{1/4}$" narrow gauge railway from the site of the former station to the lake. Whereas Nicholson's railway track was on the track bed nearest the lake side, Peter Hanton laid his track nearest the stone embankment. He submitted his plans in the autumn of 1984, and construction was underway by the end of the year. In July 1985 he commenced a railway passenger service which ran for about 300 yards, from the site of the old railway station towards the Dam; this service was extended to the Dam by Easter 1986, further along to "Lakeside" in August 1988 and eventually, in October 1992, to a terminus further along the lake, at Hunthouse Wood, a site directly opposite to the Rudyard Lake Sailing Club - a distance of approximately $1^{1/2}$ miles. The locomotives in use are 2 diesels, 2 steam and 1 petrol. Services operate throughout the year on fine weekends, and during the school holidays the train service also runs during the week. Passenger numbers have risen to around 12,000 per annum.

The Sea Scouts continued their activities during the Second World War, when their number rose to around 20. Since Mr Moreton was unable to obtain the required petrol to enable him to drive from Macclesfield to the lake, the Sea Scouts looked after the bungalow for him. After the war, he was paid a peppercorn rent, which continued until 1959, when the Sea Scouts purchased the land and building for £400. In 1964 a hut was constructed, using redundant temporary war-time classrooms from St John's School, Hanley; this was a most valuable addition, serving as both accommodation and boat store and workshop. In 1976, the Rudyard site became a recognised Royal Yachting Association training centre and during the late 1970s and the 1980s, using the old Moreton bungalow and the new hut, the Sea Scouts ran over 20 sailing courses at Rudyard; those for outsiders were held over three weekends of concentrated instruction, while others for local members were spread throughout the summer sailing season. As the old bungalow grew increasingly decrepit it was decided to replace it with a new one. Called "The Ridgway". after Sea Scout veteran Jim Ridgway, the newly built bungalow was officially opened on 26 September 1992 by Peter Moxon, the County Commissioner for Scouts. Interestingly, Peter Moxon is a direct descendant of John Munro, who built Fair View in 1880. Sadly, "The Ridgway" was burnt down in October 1993, but its replacement, by dint of much hard work, was opened in August 1994; since then it has proved very popular with outside groups such as canoeists, as well as the 89th's own Beavers, Cubs, Scouts and Venturers, who now number 65.

The Potteries Paddlers Canoeing Club, founded in 1984, established itself at Rudyard in 1986/87. Since then it has expanded progressively and now has 70 paid up members and 30 others who are connected with the Club, and there is a considerable family involvement. Membership is drawn from Leek, Congleton, Stafford and Stone, in addition to the Potteries; the enjoyment of canoeing for those with disabilities is actively promoted, The canoeing season runs from the final week of April until the first week of August, with canoeing taking place on weekday evenings. Weekend sessions are held on a monthly basis. The Club has a reputation for being extremely well organised and is noted for the skills of its trained instructors and for its excellent safety record.

The northern end of the lake is a rich location for wildlife and designation as a Site of Special Scientific Interest is currently being sought. The lake and reed beds play host to many wading birds, including heron, curlew, crested grebe, Canada goose, moorhen and many varieties of duck. Kingfishers nest in the banks and can occasionally be glimpsed in flight on fine days. During the winter months the lake becomes a birdwatcher's paradise. On autumn evenings the Rudyard skies are noisy with huge "V" shaped flights of geese. Around the time of the autumn and vernal equinox it is often possible to spot unusual migrant birds which have been blown off course.

The surrounding woodlands also support a wealth of wildlife. The greater spotted woodpecker is fairly common - often seen and frequently heard, the unmistakable 'drilling' sound echoes through the woods on still mornings. The larger green woodpecker is also occasionally seen. Nuthatches populate the larger trees in abundance, together with the tiny, mouselike treecreeper, which spirals the tree trunks in search of insects. Most varieties of finch and tit reside around the lake area, together with jays and magpies, the latter two species holding extremely noisy 'parliaments' as autumn gets underway. Tiny, brightly coloured goldcrests gather in the hedgerows of Reacliffe during the late spring and early summer. Down at ground level, the silent and patient observer may be rewarded by sight of the foxes, badgers and hedgehogs which venture forth at dusk.

The lake area offers many opportunities for botany students from nearby universities, and for members of the Staffordshire Wildlife Trust. Himalayan Balsam - probably an escapee from Victorian gardens - grows in great profusion along the edges of Reacliffe Road, and wild scabious, oxalis, celandine, purple vetch, valerian, speedwell, toadflax, wild honeysuckle and dog roses decorate the hedgerows during the springtime and summer months.

For many years there was a prevailing feeling of neglect, by the British Waterways Board, of the various users of Rudyard lake. Early in 1989, the Rudyard Lake Users' Forum was established - a body of individuals, each representing a particular group of lake users with many diverse interests, including lake management, angling, water sports, walking, nature study, bird watching, local residents and landowners. Their main concerns focus upon the future of the lake and its environs. As a forum it continues to maintain the impetus to voice the opinions of its members, but sadly it was powerless to act upon many of its concerns. At a meeting on 19 July 1994 the Rudyard Lake Users' Forum was advised by British Waterways that the Ranger service, to which, in a large part, they contributed, would have to come to an end, since their 'pump priming' exercise had not been successful. It was stated that the main concern of the British Waterways Board was the provision of water for the canal system and they requested any suggestions as to the possible future management of the lake. The Forum established its own action plan, building on an independent report commissioned by British Waterways in 1992, which led to the formation of a Limited Company, Rudyard Lake Limited on 19 April 1995, which appointed its own full-time manager, John Davey, in place of the previous ranger, Mike Booth, whom British Waterways had withdrawn in the summer of 1994. Rudyard Lake Limited's objectives are to conserve for the public benefit the natural environment of Rudyard reservoir and its surrounding area and to advance the education of the public. The appointment of a new ranger has led to more aggressive marketing of the opportunities available for fishing. Currently, around 90 angling clubs enjoy the use of the lake, coming from as far afield as Sheffield, Preston, Chester, St Helen's. Burnley and Holyhead; the transfer in November 1996 of a large number of fish from nearby Knypersley Pool will ensure attractive angling prospects for the future.

This company was the forerunner of the Rudyard Lake Trust, established in September 1996 as a Charitable Trust, on which sit 8 trustees representing British Waterways, Staffordshire Moorlands District Council, the Staffordshire Wildlife Trust and the Users' Forum. The objects of the Trust are to conserve for the public benefit the natural environment of Rudyard reservoir and its surrounding area, ensuring that it can be enjoyed not only now, but also in the longer term, and to encourage public interest in the proud 200 year history of Rudyard Lake.

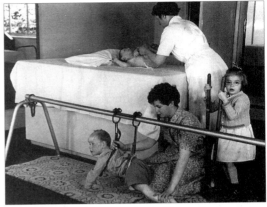

Horton Lodge School for delicate children opened in 1950 and this is a view of the original staff employed there.
Horton Lodge Special School

Children undergoing therapy at Horton Lodge in the 1950s. The Lodge was purchased in 1950 by Stoke-on-Trent City Council for the treatment of children with special needs, many of whom suffered from cerebral palsy. It is now managed by Staffordshire County Council as a Special School for children with disabilities. *Horton Lodge Special School*

The cottages on Dunwood Lane, seen here in the early 1950s, are amongst the oldest properties at Harper's Gate.
Cooper family collection

Lake Road in the early 1950s, with The Beeches on the left and the Woodside Café sign in the centre. This view shows barely any change from the earlier Edwardian postcard view on page 71.
Cooper family collection

Rudyard Lake Garage in the mid 1950s. It was built by Tom Brookes in 1929 and owned by William Abberley from c1936 to 1971.   *Fred Abberley collection*

The first Annual Dinner of the Hotel Rudyard Angling Club 1954.
L to R: Bill Hall, -, Teddy Chamberlain (Landlord of Hotel Rudyard), Barney Doyle, Herbert Lamprey, - .
Bill Hall collection

A mid 1950s view of Maynard's boats at the Dam. The Maynard family operated the boating concession from 1946 until 1969.
Colin Maynard collection

The "Rudyard Queen", the other former lifeboat purchased from Birkenhead by George Maynard in 1946. This is a mid 1950s photograph; note the merry-go-round and swings in the background, at the head of the Dam.
Colin Maynard collection

The "Rudyard Princess" seen here in the mid 1950s, about to depart from the landing stage for a trip around the lake. This was the second boat to be operated by the Maynards that had previously seen service as a lifeboat.
Colin Maynard collection

The Leek to Rudyard bus trundles under the railway bridge on 17 June 1957. The lengthened platforms can be seen on either side of the bridge. The right hand notice board directs passengers under the bridge to the adjoining walkway; "TO PLATFORM FOR PASSENGERS HOLDING TICKETS FOR LEEK AND STATIONS ONWARD". *Norman Jones*

A rail special, hauled by 2-6-0 42922 "Crab" locomotive, seen here at Rudyard lake station on 9 May 1959. Note the extended platform, visible behind the houses (built c1929), which extended from the bridge; By the early 1920s the original platform had been extended to cater for the increase in excursion traffic. Rudyard Garage is just visible on the left. *Hugh B Oliver*

Rudyard Lake station 17 June 1957, looking north, in immaculate condition with the platforms swept, the edges and verges regularly whitewashed and the delightful gardens well maintained and tended. *Norman Jones*

Harper's Gate crossroads in the late 1950s, taken from the side of the Station Hotel. Beyond the old shop property can be seen what now known as Camrose Hall, beneath which were two shops - Ellerton's the greengrocers on the left and Salt's, which operated as a café, on the right. Partially visible up the bank is the former Wesleyan Chapel, which was used for worship from 1862 to 1912. Holly Bank, as Camrose Hall was previously known, was built by Hugh Sleigh in 1891, and initially let for holiday appartments. *Cooper family collection*

The face at Rudyard Lake station in the early 1950s, thought to be that of Alexander Barnett, station master during the 1870s and 1880s.   *Author's collection*

The arrival of the only surviving Tiger Moth seaplane to Rudyard lake in the summer of 1979. Fully restored, bright red in colour, the little plane spent the entire weekend flying up and down the lake, landing and taking off from the Sailing Club. Vast crowds turned out to watch, gathering both at the Sailing Club and also massing on the main Leek to Macclesfield Road at the viewing point near the garage. The plane departed early on the Monday morning, flying past the boathouses at balcony level, to the delight of the residents.   *Christine Pemberton*

Rudyard Lake Sailing Club members preparing to sail their dinghies on a summer weekend in the 1960s

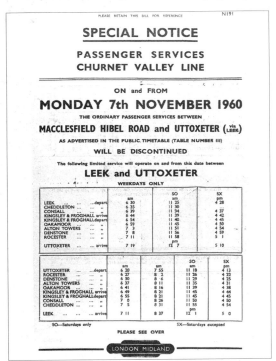

PLEASE RETAIN THIS BILL FOR REFERENCE N191

SPECIAL NOTICE

PASSENGER SERVICES CHURNET VALLEY LINE

ON and FROM

MONDAY 7th NOVEMBER 1960

THE ORDINARY PASSENGER SERVICES BETWEEN

MACCLESFIELD HIBEL ROAD and UTTOXETER (via LEEK)

AS ADVERTISED IN THE PUBLIC TIMETABLE (TABLE NUMBER III)

WILL BE DISCONTINUED

The following limited service will operate on and from this date between

LEEK and UTTOXETER

WEEKDAYS ONLY

	am	SO am	SX pm
LEEK ...depart	6 30	11 25	4 28
CHEDDLETON ... "	6 35	11 30	
CONSALL ... "	6 39	11 34	4 37
KINGSLEY & FROGHALL arrive	6 44	11 39	4 42
KINGSLEY & FROGHALL depart	6 54	11 40	4 45
OAKAMOOR ... "	6 59	11 45	4 50
ALTON TOWERS ... "	7 3	11 51	4 54
DENSTONE ... "	7 8	11 56	4 59
ROCESTER ... "	7 11	11 58	5 1
		pm	
UTTOXETER ... arrive	7 19	12 7	5 10

	am	am	SO	SX pm
UTTOXETER ...depart	6 20	7 55	11 18	4 13
ROCESTER ... "	6 27	8 2	11 26	4 22
DENSTONE ... "	6 30	8 6	11 29	4 25
ALTON TOWERS ... "	6 37	8 11	11 35	4 31
OAKAMOOR ... "	6 41	8 16	11 39	4 38
KINGSLEY & FROGHALL arrive	6 49	8 21	11 45	4 44
KINGSLEY & FROGHALL depart	6 55	8 21	11 45	4 45
CONSALL ... "	7 0	8 26	11 50	4 50
CHEDDLETON ... "	7 5	8 31	11 55	4 54
			pm	
LEEK ... arrive	7 11	8 37	12 1	5 0

SO—Saturdays only   SX—Saturdays excepted

PLEASE SEE OVER

LONDON MIDLAND

The closure notice of the Churnet Valley Line, which resulted in Rudyard Lake and Cliffe Park Halt stations being closed on 5 November 1960. *Author's collection*

Water bailiff Ivan Nixon, seen here in 1961 with the British Waterways motor boat made available for him and the Waterways Police to stop boat owners and water skiers from excessive speeding on the lake. *Ivan Nixon collection*

Miniature railway services, operated by Peter Hanton along the trackbed of the former railway, now run for 1¹/₂ miles along the eastern side of Rudyard lake, on a 10¹/₄ narrow gauge track. Seen here is a steam locomotive, the "*River Churnet*", in the spring of 1994.
Peter Hanton collection

Sam Singer and Sam Mansell have rowed the lake together every Sunday morning for the past 50 years. Here they are seen at the official opening, on Sunday 7 April 1996. of the new access to the foreshore.
Leek Post and Times

This book has been assisted by
Britannia Building Society

Britannia was originally established in 1856 as the Leek and Moorlands Building Society, a name it retained until 1956 when following a merger with the Westbourne Park Building Society it became the Leek and Westbourne. Another merger with Eastern Counties Building Society meant a name change to the Leek Westbourne & Eastern Counties. The name Britannia was finally adopted in 1975, after more than sixty mergers.

Today Britannia is the sixth largest UK building society, with Group assets exceeding £14.5 billion. The Society currently has 199 branch offices around the country. In addition to the branch network, the Society has also developed a highly successful postal investment service and three further distribution channels: a financial planning service, an intermediary sales force and telephone marketing.

Following the proposed and actual conversion to plc status of a number of building societies, Britannia has emerged as one of the leading advocates of retaining its mutual status. In support of this stance, Britannia announced the launch of a unique Members' Loyalty Bonus Scheme in February 1996. Through the scheme, the Society's 1.6 million members will share the profits of the organisation through annual cash payouts, so that we can truly call ourselves the "Sharing Society".